Managing Your Household Well

Preparation for Aspiring Elders and Pastors

Daryl Kroeker
and
Richard Magill

Unless otherwise noted, all Scripture quotations are taken from the ESV® Bible (The Holy Bible, English Standard Version®) copyright © 2001 by Crossway, a publishing ministry of Good News Publishers. Used by permission. All rights reserved.

Cover Image: This cover has been designed using images from Flaticon.com

WorldServe Ministries
PO Box 39530 RPO White Rock
Surrey, BC V4A 0A9
Canada
1.800.414.7788

ISBN: 978-1-7781310-1-1

Dedicated
to
Melissa Magill
and
Tamara Kroeker
who patiently
walk with us
as we
stumble towards
managing our households well.

Special thanks to
Dorothy Isted
and
Barbara Burchert
for their editorial skills
that helped
make this book possible.

Table of Contents

How To Use This Book

This book has two types of men in mind. First, it is for those who aspire to be leaders within the church family. The Bible refers to these men as elders and deacons. The elders are those who are responsible for the oversight and teaching in the church family. The deacons are generally responsible for the delivery of ministry. Both are told they are to manage their households well (1 Timothy 3:5 and 3:12). If you are among those who desire to meet the qualifications of an elder or deacon, you desire a noble thing (1 Timothy 3:1). But before you can assume the task, you must meet the qualifications outlined by Paul in his letters to Timothy and Titus. Our prayer is that this book will help you assess where you currently are, make you aware of the areas in which you need to grow, and help you develop the tools and strategies you need to push toward spiritual maturity.

The second type of man this book seeks to address is one who is already serving in a position of leadership. You may be serving as a volunteer leader, or your service may be vocational. You may already be a deacon, and elder or a pastor. Our desire is that this book will help you evaluate how you are doing and make you aware of the areas of your life that need further growth.

This book is not designed to be simply read. It is designed as a discipleship tool. To benefit the most, you need to take time to read each chapter and work through the questions and activities included at the end of each chapter. You may want to do this by yourself, but we feel it would be better to do this with another person or group of people so that you can grow together and keep each other accountable for progress.

Preface

As I (Richard) write this I must confess, I am angry. Just days ago, an independent team of investigators announced their findings after an in-depth investigation into numerous allegations of sexual misconduct against pastors and ministry leaders in a major global denomination. Upon the report's release, the denomination has agreed to release a list of over 700 pastors that have been accused of sexual misconduct: a list that has heretofore been kept secret for over two decades.[1] In an apparently unrelated incident, a pastor in Indiana closed out his sermon on repentance this past Sunday by confessing that he had had an affair twenty years ago. The victim, still a member of the congregation, walked to the microphone to correct him. She reported that the affair actually began twenty seven years ago when she was 16 years old, and it lasted for nine years.[2] These two incidents, both happening just days before I began to think seriously about this project, serve to bring back recollections of numerous, far too many, similar high-profile cases over the last several decades. And for every high-profile case of sexual abuse made public we can be certain there are dozens, and even hundreds, of pastors and ministry leaders from smaller churches falling into sexual misconduct that we never hear about.

I am angry and I am weary. Sexual misconduct among clergy and other ministry leaders is grievous, but it is only a symptom of a much larger, systemic problem in the church: a problem that has

---

[1] Ruth Graham, "Southern Baptists to Release List of Ministers Accused of Sexual Abuse," *The New York Times,* Last modified May 24, 2022, https://www.nytimes.com/2022/05/24/us/southern-baptist-sexual-abuse.html.

[2] Johnathon Edwards, "Pastor Confessed to Adultery. The Woman Cried out, 'I was just 16.'" *The Washington Post,* Last modified May 24, 2022, https://www.washingtonpost.com/nation/2022/05/24/pastor-confesses-adultery-teenager/.

yet more symptoms than just sexual misconduct. As I write this, I am thinking of a half a dozen men or more from the American mega-church movement who were once household names in the American church (and often the world) but have taken epic falls because of their pride in the last few decades. Pride that is often manifest in dictatorship styles of leadership, frequent fits of rage when they didn't get their way or someone dared disagree with them, and a long trail of colleagues, subordinates, and congregants left broken and hurt in their wake. And yet again, for every fall of a high-profile pastor, so many men of similar character have fallen for similar reasons on a smaller scale apart from the public eye.

And then there are those pastors and church leaders that are leaving the ministry, some even the church, at an almost epidemic rate due to fatigue and burnout these last few years. It draws tears to my eyes every time I hear a ministry leader I deeply respect make the comment, "I'm deconstructing my faith." Ministry is hard; Daryl and I are well aware of the fact that anyone reading this book knows that.

For those of you reading this book with future aspirations of becoming an elder, pastor, or church leader, this book is about preparation. I hope this book compels you to ask yourself:

- Am I really called by God Himself, to be a pastor or elder? How can I know?
- Do I have the heart, the passions and desires of a pastor or elder? Are my motivations that of a ministry leader called by God to care for His sheep?
- Do I have the character of a pastor or elder?
- Do I have the qualifications of a pastor or elder?
- Do I have the spiritual discipline of a pastor or elder?

For the aspiring pastor, this is a book about preparation – and it is about prevention. These questions are questions that must be answered well and wisely long before entering the ministry if you are to have any hope of avoiding the above-mentioned, or countless other pitfalls that would ultimately drive you to a crash, bring much damage to the body of Christ, and, more importantly, defame the name of the Lord Jesus.

This book is a wake-up call for those already in ministry. None of those pastors entered the ministry expecting to be disqualified a few years or decades later by moral failure or weak character. I am confident many truly have a relationship with Jesus and entered the ministry, at least in part, because they desired to invite others into relationship with Him. Their falls were actually the result of a million little compromises in morality and discipline that led to their ultimate demise. Perhaps they:

- Entered the ministry prematurely, before they were ready.
- Entered the ministry for the wrong reasons.
- Harbored a secret fantasy life that finally forced its way to the surface.
- Allowed their priorities, values, and passions to be dictated by desires and persons other than Christ and the precious truths of the gospel.

For those already in ministry this book is a wake-up call… and it's an assessment tool. It reminds us of the Biblical qualifications for the church leader and invites us to measure ourselves and our ministry practices against it. Where do I need help? Where do I fall short? For what do I need to repent? What gifts and blessings has God given me, that I might help our flock and other ministry leaders?

One last note – if you have the courage to measure yourself and your ministry against the Bible you WILL fall short. Even as I begin to think through the scope and scale of this project, the sense of hypocrisy that I would be a part of it threatens to crush me. Please read this book with the following in mind. I in no way see myself as a great guru of ministry, wise beyond his years in the ways of pastoral leadership. Quite the opposite. I feel wholly unqualified and unworthy to participate in this project. I love my God, but all too often I allow other loves to crowd out my love for Him. I love my wife, but far from perfectly. I love the congregation which God has charged me to care for and strive to do so intentionally. But more often than I care to admit, I feel like I often do not know what I am doing. I am tired and too often seek rest in frivolous, pointless or even dangerous things. I teach that Christ is the only path to our salvation and yet I run to the altars of numerous false saviors more times than even I realize.

This book is for the aspiring and existing ministry leader, but first it's for me. I need to be reminded repeatedly of my calling, character, and qualifications as a pastor. I also need to be reminded of how short I fall in all three areas. In other words, I desperately need Jesus. That's what repentance is for. That's what the cross takes care of. While Scripture does tell us that ministry leaders will be held to a higher standard (James 3:1), that does not mean that we are in any less need of the gospel truths that we teach those under our care. In some senses, perhaps we need His grace more so.

One of the main qualifications of being a ministry leader is a recognition that apart from His grace we are wholly unqualified to mention His name, much less proclaim His glory to the world and invite them to do the same. If Christ's proclamation to Paul in 2 Corinthians 12:9 is true, *My grace is sufficient for you, for my power is perfected in weakness,* then we must constantly be aware of and confessing our weaknesses and failures to God and others if we are ever going to be truly successful as His children, much less as ministry leaders. One of the primary purposes of this book is to call us all into a lifestyle of repentance so that we may never find ourselves too exhausted to continue or to be disqualified from doing the ministry that we love and are called to.

Introduction

My wife and I (Daryl) seem quite normal. At least it seems that way to us. We have two married children – a boy, and a girl. From these two have sprung twelve grandchildren. We are still not sure how our limited fruitfulness could swell to that number, but it did. Both our son and son-in-law are serving in full-time pastoral ministry.

We have been asked many times to disclose the secret or key to our apparent family success. This has left us perplexed because we could not think of a specific strategy or key that we could point others to. Except, perhaps one: the grace of God.

It has been God's gracious favor and kindness to us that is evidenced again and again in our family. We made many mistakes along the way, but it was God's grace that granted us forgiveness over and over. It was God's grace that called our children to himself. It was God's grace that captured their hearts and sent them on their journey towards the gates of glory. We are now praying that God's grace will do the same in each of our precious grandchildren.

Lest you think that my wife and I floundered our way through marriage and family life, you need to know we did seek to build our marriage and family on the foundation of God's word. While we stumbled often, it was our desire to submit to the leadership of the Holy Spirit as he led and strengthened us to obey the principles found on the pages of the Bible. I suppose the key to our family would be God's grace, and our reliance on the Holy Spirit to change us to be more and more obedient to the will of God found in the authoritative word of God, the Bible.

With this in mind, we turn to 1 Timothy 3:4 where Paul tells Timothy that an elder, or a leader among God's people, *must manage his own household well.* This phrase is found in the context of Paul's letter to Timothy where he is given instructions on how to lead the church in Ephesus. Timothy is called on to confront false teachers, teach sound doctrine and prepare men for elder and deacon leadership in the church.

What does it mean to manage a household well? What does this look like? Why was this the measurement used to determine who qualified to serve as an elder?

To understand the breadth of this measurement, we need to first understand the word *household.* In Greek, the original language of the New Testament, this is the word *oikos.* This word was used of a building, of the people who lived there, and of the people who were connected to the people who lived there. In biblical times a household would include more than a single family. It would be more than a husband, wife, and children. It included both those who made a particular building their home and those who were connected to that home, including servants, employees, extended family and others within their circle of influence.[3]

If we use the household concept from Paul, our *oikos* today would include our family, our neighbors, our contacts at work and the people we regularly interact with outside of our work. If we were to divide this into circles of influence, there would most likely be two. Within our household we have a primary sphere of influence which would include our close family and friends. Our secondary circle of influence would include the people we work with, our acquaintances and casual relationships.

What does this all mean? Simply this: To manage our household well means that God expects we manage each of these relational connections according to the principles found in his

---

[3] J. P. Louw and Eugene A. Nida, eds., *Greek-English Lexicon of the New Testament: Based on Semantic Domains,* 1st ed. (New York, NY, USA: United Bible Societies, 1988), 113.

Word. The purpose of this book is to help us with that task.

The Bible and Cultural Differences

Whenever we study the Bible, our intent is to discover the biblical principles, commands and promises that transcend time and culture. We want to discover what God is saying to all people during any time and in any culture. These are the principles that are true in North America, South America, Europe, Africa and Asia. They are the directives from God that need to be followed wherever in the world we live.

How they are applied to your family or church might be different than how we might apply them to our family and church. The goal is not to make us all look alike and like the same things. The goal is to discern from God's Word what he would have us be like so we may reflect his glory in the community in which he has placed us.

How you apply the principles you will discover from the Bible will be up to you and the Holy Spirit. At the end of each section, there will be several application questions that will help you employ the principles in your life and circumstance.

A Model for Godly Men

1 Timothy 3 gives us the criteria that is to be used in choosing elders in the church. To help him choose elders or overseers of the church carefully, Paul gives Timothy these instructions:

> *The saying is trustworthy: If anyone aspires to the office of overseer, he desires a noble task. Therefore an overseer must be above reproach, the husband of one wife, sober-minded, self-controlled, respectable, hospitable, able to teach, not a drunkard, not violent but gentle, not quarrelsome, not a lover of money. He must manage his own household well, with all dignity keeping his children submissive, for if someone*

does not know how to manage his own household, how will he care for God's church? He must not be a recent convert, or he may become puffed up with conceit and fall into the condemnation of the devil. Moreover, he must be well thought of by outsiders, so that he may not fall into disgrace, into a snare of the devil.

This list of qualifications for church leadership gives us the description of a man who is a mature believer. The instruction is quite simple: When choosing church leaders, you look to the most mature men in the church family.

It is important to notice this list is not a job description, but a character list. It does not tell us everything that a pastor, elder or church leader is to do. But it does tell us what their life is to look like. Because ministry leadership is a noble task it comes with specific qualifications. It is not just for anyone, but for a specific type of person.

This list contains thirteen character qualities. The mature man is to be:

- Above reproach
- The husband of one wife
- Sober-minded
- Self-controlled
- Respectable
- Hospitable
- Gentle
- Well thought of by outsiders.

He is not to be:

- A drunkard
- Violent
- Quarrelsome
- A lover of money

- A recent convert to the faith

There are two items on the list that tell us what this church leader is supposed to be able to do.

1. He is to be able to teach
2. He must manage his own household well

It is on this last qualification we want to focus our attention. Paul very clearly says in verses 4 and 5,

> *He must manage his own household well, with all dignity keeping his children submissive, for if someone does not know how to manage his own household, how will he care for God's church?*

By focusing on this we will also speak to the other qualifications on the list.

Perhaps you are reading this book because you are already in or are preparing for leadership within the context of the local church. That leadership position comes with all kinds of responsibilities and challenges. There are people who need to be taught. There are people who need to be encouraged. Some are broken and hurting. Some need to be discipled. Some need to be listened to and cared for. Some need a model to follow.

Though we can go to school to learn how to shepherd the church of God. It is interesting that the Bible tells us that training to be a leader is not found in a Bible school or seminary but in the home. While a good Bible education is very valuable, the proving or testing ground of our ability to be a leader is found in the management of our own household.

What we are in our household is what we really are. How we lead and care for our wife and children and the people around us is how we will lead and care for the church family.

Failure in this area of leadership is often at the root of leadership failure in the church. Poor fathering, consistently rebellious children, a failing marriage and broken relationships all say something about our ability to provide leadership in the church family.

Why Do We Need to Manage Our Household Well?

There are six significant reasons for managing our household well.

1. **At creation the family was established by God** (Genesis 1-2).

   The family is God's means of propagating the human species. The family is God's design and is the primary training ground for life's interactions. Every single life that is ever lived – whether good or bad – begins in a familial relationship. This is the way God meant it to be. This is the first responsibility of man – to care for and lead his family.

   Not only is the family God's means of propagating the species, but it is also God's primary means by which he provides the solution for the most profound problem that mankind has ever faced: loneliness. When we read, *Then the LORD God said, 'It is not good that man should be alone…,'* our jaws are meant to drop! What on earth would be so profoundly wrong, so profoundly bad, that God, who has so far spent the entirety of His creative act remarking on how good everything is (cf: Genesis 1)? What would cause Him to stop in His tracks and proclaim, "now that… that is NOT good"?

   Of course, Genesis 2:18 goes on to answer, *"that man should not be alone; I will make a helper fit for him."* In other words, the most profound problem mankind has ever faced is loneliness. God spends verses 19 and 20 of Chapter 2 convincing Adam that there is no solution to his loneliness, either within himself or anywhere on earth. After Adam has named all the existing animals (searching for a "helper fit for him"), there is a rather depressing comment made at the end of Genesis 2:20: "*…but for Adam there was not found a helper fit for him.*" It would take nothing short of a miracle handed down directly from the hand of God to solve his profound problem of loneliness. That miracle takes the form of Eve, to which Adam composes the first love song: "*Then the man said, 'This at last is bone of my bones and flesh of my flesh; she shall be called Woman, because she was taken out of Man'*" (Gen. 2:23). In other words, family is the primary solution to our loneliness.

Never allow yourself to believe the lie that you can fix your loneliness yourself. Your loneliness is a God-sized problem that requires a God-sized solution; a solution that God has already provided through family. When we forget that, we are headed down the path toward all types of dangerous territory. It is here, in our desire to fix our God-sized problem of loneliness without God, that a lascivious fantasy life, masturbation, physical relationships outside of marriage, pornography and other forms of sexual addiction, homosexuality and gender fluidity and the like all find fertile ground to grow. Sometimes these things take years, even decades, to cultivate into fruition. But they first find root in our desire to try to fix a problem that only God can fix: our loneliness; a problem that God has *already* fixed – through family.

2. The role relationships in a marriage are a picture of the Trinity of God.

Marriage relationships are a wonderful display of the relationship between authority and submission as seen in God himself. While being totally equal, the members of the Trinity display relationships of authority and submission. The Son came to do the will of the Father and in so doing submits to the Father even though all things were made by him, through him and for him. The Holy Spirit submits to the Son in that his task is to glorify the Son. Yet they are equally one God.

In the same way, authority and submission in the family has nothing to do with one person's superiority and another's inferiority. While all people, husbands and wives, parents and children have different roles that call for authority and submission, they do not make people inferior to one another just as the members of the Trinity exercise authority and submission but are not inferior to one another.

One way for people to understand and see the glory of the Triune God is through the example of a husband and wife who live in a godly authority and submission relationship.[4]

3.   **The family is how God tells his story**.

God uses the family as a primary means of revealing his character, his grace, and his plan for redemption. We see his hand in the story of Abraham, Isaac, Jacob, and their family. It is through Israel's history we see the story of every human heart and the glory of God's redemption.

As the Old Testament narrative unfolds, we see the tale told on three levels. The upper level is the grand story of God's sovereign redemptive work which moves all of history toward the cross where sin is atoned for and then from the cross toward the glorious return of Christ. History exists to reveal God. It is all about Him.

The middle level portrays the call of Abraham to be the family through which God would work to accomplish redemption. John Piper writes,

"Israel is the historical theatre where the drama of every

---

[4] For a fuller discussion see Bruce A. Ware, *Father, Son, and Holy Spirit: Relationships, Roles, and Relevance* (Wheaton, Ill: Crossway Books, 2005), 131–151.

human soul is played out for all to see. What goes on inside you spiritually – and every other person – has gone on in Israel historically, and the story is told so we can see ourselves and the world. If you want to know your own spiritual condition before God as a human being – if you want to know the greatest issues for the world – you can learn it from watching the history of Israel as it is interpreted in the Bible."[5]

The bottom level of the story is made up of the accounts of individuals and families through whom God worked to accomplish his grand narrative.

Even today, your family is important. Your marriage is important. It is part of the grand narrative of God whereby he tells the story of his love and grace and call to redemption and forgiveness. Your family is one of the means God uses to call people in your community to himself. Your family is a picture of what God can do when he redeems, renews, and rebuilds broken lives. Your family is the tool God will use to tell and illustrate his story in your community. At least we hope it is.

4. **Marriage is a picture of the relationships between Christ and His followers** (Ephesians 5).

Ephesians 5 makes it very clear that husbands are to *love their wives as Christ loved the church and gave himself up for her*. It is the picture of Christ's absolute sacrifice of everything for the redemption of mankind. It is the picture of selfless love.

As the wife submits to her husband it is the picture of Christ's submission to the Father and a picture of the church's submission

---

[5] John Piper, "The Word of Faith That We Proclaim, Part 1," *Desiring God*, last modified May 18, 2003, accessed May 23, 2022, https://www.desiringgod.org/messages/the-word-of-faith-that-we-proclaim-part-1.

to the leadership of Christ.

Satan loves to destroy this picture. According to Revelation 12 we face the rage of Satan. He knows his time is short (12:10-12), his sphere of influence is restricted (12:13), and his success is limited (12:14-16). And he is furious!

He is already defeated, but he is determined to do as much damage as possible and to take as many people with him as possible. And our marriages are often in the center of that battle! Satan knows if he can destroy this very practical picture, if he can destroy your marriage, he can destroy the reputation of the church and of Christ.

5. **Our family gives a picture of ministry relationships** (1 Thessalonians 2:1-12; 1 Timothy 5:1-2).

Paul spoke of ministering among people as a mother and a father.

> *We were gentle among you like a nursing mother taking care of her own children. So, being affectionately desirous of you, we were ready to share with you not only the gospel of God but also our own selves, because you had become very dear to us.* (1 Thessalonians 2:7-8)

> *For you know how, like a father with his children, we exhorted each one of you and encouraged you and charged you to walk in a manner worthy of God, who calls you into his own kingdom and glory.* (1 Thessalonians 2:11-12)

1 Timothy 3:15 calls the church *the household of God.* If we do not know how to manage our own household, how can we know how to minister to others as fathers and mothers?

6. **Marriage and family relationships are the proving ground for potential church leadership** (1 Timothy 3:1-5; 3:10-12; Titus 1:6).

This brings us back to 1 Timothy 3:5, *"if someone does not know how to manage his own household, how will he care for God's church?"* If we cannot lead and manage our own families, we do not qualify to serve as an elder, overseer or pastor in the family of God. Our home relationships need to be biblically managed before a church ministry assignment can be given. The one crucial evidence of fitness for being an overseer in the family of God is that a man manages his own natural family well.

The word "manage" has two dimensions of meaning. It means to "stand before" either as one who leads or as one who protects and provides. It is the latter that is the focus of this verse because at the end of the verse, Paul talks about caring for God's church.

The aim of church leadership is not coercion, but care. In Luke 22:26 Jesus said, *"Let the greatest among you become as the youngest, and the leader as one who serves."* How a man manages or cares for his own family is a good test of whether he will provide the caring leadership the church needs.

The Bible does not address how to choose elders and pastors. But in Paul's day their appointment to the office and task was based on these qualifications. Today some churches appoint, some elect, but that is not the issue here in the text. The process of choosing leaders can look very different in different cultures, but the qualifications remain the same. All over the world, elders should be men who manage their household well.

If you want to know how someone will lead the church of God, look at his family leadership. What is his marriage like? How does he treat his wife? How does he lead and care for and train his children?

Application Questions or Activities

1. How would you measure your motive for elder or pastoral leadership? Use the chart below for your evaluation.

Motivation for Ministry

a. Motivation must not come from a desire for personal recognition or gain.

... People who want to get rich fall into temptation and a trap and into many foolish and harmful desires that plunge men into ruin and destruction. (1 Tim. 6:9)

... Some people, eager for money, have wandered from the faith and pierced themselves with many griefs. (1 Tim. 6:10)

Weak				Strong
1	2	3	4	5

b. Motivation must come from godly character not worldly comfort.

... But you, man of God, flee from all this, and pursue righteousness, godliness, faith, love, endurance, and gentleness. (1 Tim. 6:11)

... Fight the good fight of the faith. (1 Tim. 6:12)

... Take hold of the eternal life to which you were called when you made your good confession in the presence of many witnesses. (1 Tim. 6:12)

Weak				Strong
1	2	3	4	5

c. Motivation must be willingness to lead rather than drive.

... Be shepherds of God's flock that is under your care, serving as overseers

... not because you must, but because you are willing, as God wants you to be.

... not greedy for money, but eager to serve;

... not lording it over those entrusted to you, but being examples to the flock. (1 Peter 5:2-3)

Weak				Strong
1	2	3	4	5

2. As you review the qualities outlined above how do you measure up? Has a lack in any of these areas disqualified you until you are able to make significant progress? Where do you need to keep growing? What do you need to do to progress toward godliness in these areas? What are you going to do?

3. What is the most significant thing you learned from this introduction?

4. We have all felt lonely; we all will again. In what ways are you most often tempted to "fix" your loneliness apart from God? It is an important question, as it will probably be one of the primary ways in which Satan tempts you away from the character, discipline, and qualifications of a pastor, elder or church leader.

5. What sin patterns and character flaws in you and your wife threaten your marriage? Is there any biblical teaching that you find hard to believe and/or submit to? If you are single, what do you need to work on as preparation for marriage?

6. If you aspire to be a leader in your church family, which of the character qualities would your wife or children agree that you have? Which would they say you need to grow in?

7. If you are single, where have your closest friends, spiritual mentors and church leaders affirmed you? Challenged you?

8. As you begin this study, are you courageous enough to ask

the Lord to speak into your life and give you a listening mind and an eager heart to respond to Him?

9. Who are you willing to enlist to help you continue to grow? Besides your wife, who are you willing to be vulnerable with and accountable to in this journey? Be sure to talk to them and invite them to walk with you.

Chapter 1: You

As you prepare to lead your household well – and subsequently the church family – you need to know that household management must begin with self-management. To manage your household well, you need to begin with you.

Self-examination is hard. It is much easier to point out the flaws, problems, and failures of others. They are so obvious to us.

Most of us don't like to look at ourselves. We don't spend a lot of time in front of a mirror. We just take a quick glance and move on. Sometimes it is because we don't like what we see. Other times it is because we think we look good enough.

But to mature into godly men, we need to stop and linger at the mirror of God's Word. James tells us that the way to avoid being deceived about ourselves is take a long look at ourselves through the Word.

> *But be doers of the word, and not hearers only, deceiving yourselves. For if anyone is a hearer of the word and not a doer, he is like a man who looks intently at his natural face in a mirror. For he looks at himself and goes away and at once forgets what he was like. But the one who looks into the perfect law, the law of liberty, and perseveres, being no hearer who forgets but a doer who acts, he will be blessed in his doing* (James 1:22-25).

Waking Up from Sleepiness

It is easy to be sleepy or lethargic and inactive when we think about how we are doing. Most men are not very introspective. But in the book of Romans Paul tells us it is time to wake up from our sleepiness. He writes,

> *Besides this you know the time, that the hour has come for you to wake from sleep. For salvation is nearer to us now than when we first*

believed. 12 The night is far gone; the day is at hand. So then let us cast off the works of darkness and put on the armor of light. 13 Let us walk properly as in the daytime, not in orgies and drunkenness, not in sexual immorality and sensuality, not in quarreling and jealousy. 14 But put on the Lord Jesus Christ, and make no provision for the flesh, to gratify its desires (Romans 13:11-14).

To understand these verses correctly, we need to know the context of Romans. The first eleven chapters describe the glorious gospel of grace. We are declared "not guilty", our sins are forgiven, Christ's righteousness is applied to the account of our lives, we are adopted into God's family, we are given the indwelling Holy Spirit and we are on a journey of sanctification that leads to the gates of glory where we will enjoy God's riches forever!

Because of the glorious gospel of grace outlined in chapters 1-11, Paul calls us to action in chapters 12-15.

- 12:3-8 – We are called to use our spiritual gifts in serving others.
- 12:9-13 – We are called to love one another.
- 12:14-21 – We are called to bless those who persecute us.
- 13:1-7 – We are called to submit to authority over us.
- 13:8-10 – We are called again to love one another.
- 14:1-15:7 – We are called to accept those who have different convictions about living the Christian life practically.

In 13:11 Paul reminds us of the shortness of time before the return of Christ and calls us to *wake up from sleep.*

Sleepiness describes too many believers today. They are morally careless. They are undisciplined. They are spiritually lazy. They are governed by compromise with the world around them. They believe the facts of the gospel but there appears to be very little impact or change in the way they live. They remind us of the chief priests and scribes of Matthew 2, who knew exactly where the Messiah was to be born (Micah 2) but did not bother to walk the eight kilometers to investigate what the wise men from the east were seeking.

We can even find church leaders who are sleepy. They have lost the vibrancy of their love for Christ. They fulfill their church duties out of habit. They no longer seem fresh and alive with the Word of God or Spirit of God. They feel empty and tired.

As we have looked at our own lives, we have discovered there are several reasons this can happen to us:

We are tired. We have been serving without spiritual or physical refreshment. We have been doing our ministry with our own energy and we have grown tired. Too much to do. Too many people. So few resources. So little time.

We lack accountability. We have fallen asleep, and we do not have anyone to poke us awake. It is like falling asleep during a long sermon – we need someone to poke us – to get us to wake up. No one is asking us the hard questions of life. Or if they are, we are not honest with them or the Lord about our true spiritual condition. Sometimes ministry leaders and mature Christians believe that accountability is reserved for those trying to find victory over some pervasive sin or bad habit. Accountability is highly effective in that context, but it is necessary in so many other contexts. Paul Tripp has been known to say of spiritual blindness, "we are blind to our own blindness."[6] Accountability relationships see in us what we can't see in ourselves.

Familiarity. We have been a student of the Word so long that instead of refreshing our souls, it has become purely an academic

---

[6] Paul Tripp, "Blind to our Blindness," *The Gospel Coalition, Blogpost* last modified April 1st, 2012, https://www.thegospelcoalition.org/article/blind-to-our-blindness/.

exercise. Our study and sermon preparation are for someone else and not for us. Or, instead of digging into the text to discover the precious nuggets of God's truth, we take shortcuts and only use other people's material or sermons. Instead of teaching out of the wealth of our own study, we hand out the leftovers of someone else's study.

We misunderstand grace. We forget Paul's "God forbid" of Romans 6:2. Instead of seeing the depth of our sin and the greatness of God's grace; instead of seeing the daily addition to the list of sins that ought to be counted against us and rejoicing in God's grace, we take a mediocre or careless approach to the Christian life. We don't worry too much about our sin because we say God will understand, or that God knows we are weak, or that it does not really matter that much how we live if we are generally faithful. We no longer celebrate grace!

We struggle with the swing between self-righteousness and guilt. We have been told or think that to get God happy with us or to keep him happy with us we must accomplish a long list of religious activities. When we can maintain our self-contrived "To Do" list we feel smug and comfortable and think that God must be quite pleased with us. And if we are not successful, we are afflicted with guilt and wonder how God could ever forgive us or be happy with us because of our continual failure. And so we swing back and forth, back and forth until we are dizzy, or confused and disoriented and just want to forget it all and go to sleep. We have forgotten the wonder of Romans 8:28-39 and the amazing assurance that is ours.

We allow our sin nature to rule. Instead of putting to death the thoughts and deeds of darkness we allow them to lurk in the corners of our lives. Slowly the darkness closes in, and we become sleepy and hardly notice how far we have drifted from the life God has called us to.

We avoid or neglect a lifestyle of confession and repentance. We will speak more on this later, but inevitably, the lie that we need Christ's forgiveness just a little less than we used to – just a little less than those for whom we care – will creep in if we don't guard ourselves against it. We guard against it by embracing a lifestyle of repentance. Repentance is not just to "get us in the door" of Christ's family, nor is it reserved for those big sins that would make our neighbour blush if they knew we'd committed them. John Owen writes a beautiful prayer of repentance. We are quoting the original just because we love the poetry of it (for a modern paraphrase see foot note[7]):

> Bring thy lust to the gospel, —not for relief, but for further conviction of its guilt; look on Him whom thou hast pierced, and be in bitterness. Say to thy soul, "What have I done? What love, what mercy, what blood, what grace have I despised and trampled on? Is this the return I make to the Father for his love, to the Son for his blood, to the Holy Ghost for his grace?

---

[7] Next bring your evil desires to the gospel – not to soothe your guilty conscience but to make you feel even guiltier. Look at Christ crucified for your sin and let your behavior appall you. Say to yourself: What have I done? What love, what mercy, what blood, what grace have I despised and trampled on! Is this how I pay back the Father for His love, the Son for His blood, and the Holy Spirit for His grace?! Is this how I show my appreciation? Have I actually defiled the heart that Christ died to make clean and that the Holy Spirit has chosen to live in? What can I say to Lord Jesus? How can I hold my head up with any boldness in front of Him? Do I put so little value on my fellowship with Him that for the sake of this evil desire I've left Him so little room in my heart? How will I escape if I "neglect such a great salvation" (Hebrews 2:3)? How am I going to be able to explain this? Love, mercy, grace, goodness, peace, joy, comfort – I have despised them all and considered them of no value, just so I could continue to cling to sin in my heart. Did Jesus die so that I could approach confidently to the throne of grace only to enable me to insult God to His face? Did my soul get washed clean so that I could dirty it up again with fresh sin? Will I try to keep the objective of Christ's death from occurring? Will I grieve the Holy Spirit day after day when heseals me to the day of redemption? John Owen, The Mortification of Sin, Translated and Adapted into Modern English by Aaron M. Renn, (2019: TradLife Press, New York, NY), 79.

Do I thus requite the Lord? Have I defiled the heart that Christ died to wash, that the blessed Spirit hath chosen to dwell in? And can I keep myself out of the dust? What can I say to the dear Lord Jesus? How shall I hold up my head with any boldness before him? Do I account communion with him of so little value, that for this vile lust's sake I have scarce left him any room in my heart? How shall I escape if I neglect so great salvation? In the meantime, what shall I say to the Lord? Love, mercy, grace, goodness, peace, joy, consolation, – I have despised them all, and esteemed them as a thing of nought, that I might harbour a lust in my heart. Have I obtained a view of God's fatherly countenance, that I might behold his face and provoke him to his face? Was my soul washed, that room might be made for new defilements? Shall I endeavour to disappoint the end of the death of Christ? Shall I daily grieve that Spirit whereby I am sealed to the day of redemption? Entertain thy conscience daily with this.[8]

Owen understood that repentance is for every heart attitude that is not in line with the mind of Christ. In his writing, Owen uses the word "lust" in the first line as a much broader term than just sexual lust. Repentance is for every selfish desire, whether we act on it or not. It is for everything that motivates us apart from Christ's love and His commission. It is for every time I act to bring glory to myself rather than to Him. In other words, repentance is for every step of the way and as ministers of the gospel, we must embrace that lifestyle, perhaps even more than those for whom we care.

---

[8] John Owen, The Mortification of Sin in Believers. Public Domain.

In case you have not previously understood sin as quite so broad a category, or our need for continual repentance so great, here is a note of encouragement: Christ promises all-inclusive forgiveness. *If we confess our sins, he is faithful and just to forgive us our sins and will cleanse us from all unrighteousness* (1 John 1:9). No matter how big or small the sin – from a human perspective – no matter how often we go before the throne of Christ in confession, the consequence of confessing is always, always, always forgiveness. We can enter a lifestyle of repentance with joy and thanksgiving because Christ, contrary to what we deserve, has promised to always respond to our repentance with forgiveness and purification!

We have been asked on occasion when should a pastor or ministry leader be required to repent publicly? First, we would argue that there is a problem with the question. Living a lifestyle of repentance does not mean that we need to start off every service with a list of all the sins we have committed over the last week. However it does mean that we are to live so transparently and vulnerably that if we were to list off our sins, at no point would the more mature of the congregation be surprised.

For those still looking for guidance in this area, consider this – repentance should always include everyone you have sinned against. All sin is an offence against God, so all sin should be confessed to Him in repentance. If it is also against your family, repent to them as well. A friend or colleague? Go to them in repentance. If it is against your church family or your community, you must also repent to them.

Notice what Paul calls us to do in response to this sleepiness. It is found in Romans 13:12-14.

> *The night is far gone; the day is at hand. So then let us cast off the works of darkness and put on the armor of light. Let us walk properly*

as in the daytime, not in orgies and drunkenness, not in sexual immorality and sensuality, not in quarreling and jealousy. But put on the Lord Jesus Christ, and make no provision for the flesh, to gratify its desires.

There are some things we need to cast off. First, there are the sins of addiction. In reference to his culture, Paul calls them *orgies and drunkenness*. In our culture these addictions take multiple forms. In addition to alcohol and drugs, we can be addicted to television, social media, sports, news, and even food. Biblically speaking, addiction and idolatry are synonyms. Tim Keller states: "An idol is usually a good thing we make ultimate. We say, 'Unless I have that, I am nothing.'"[9] In other words, when we lean too heavily on anything – good or bad – for release, comfort, pleasure, escape, rest, we become dependent on it.

Next, Paul mentions sexual sins. He calls them *sexual immorality and sensuality*. Even among believers the use of pornography found on the internet and social media is astounding. The satisfaction of lust begins on our phone and eventually spreads like a cancer to our view of women and our interaction with them. It is shocking to learn how many young men who claim to be Christ-followers are addicted to pornography. It would also be very shocking to have our thought lives made public. We do not think it too direct to state that until someone has complete victory over their porn addiction, they are NOT ready for ministry. Yes, the Lord forgives. When we say we do not believe they are ready for ministry we are not questioning their salvation, since there is a lot more to consider before we would question whether someone has a genuine relationship with Jesus. Though we do emphatically declare – in light of Scripture – they are not ready to enter a

---

[9] Timothy Keller. *Twitter*, 16 Feb. 2014, 9:00am.,
    https://twitter.com/timkellernyc/status/435096272580911104?lang=en

profession of leading others toward salvation.

One other word of warning: We assume that most who read this book are male, so we are speaking directly to men, here. But be aware that pornography use among women is growing at an epidemic rate these days. If nothing else, men, keep that in mind as you are seeking your future wife. Some of the most toxic relationships we've ever worked with involve a husband and wife who are both addicted to porn.

Finally, in Paul's list of things to cast off, are the social or relationship sins which he describes as *quarrelling and jealousy*. Quarrelling comes from wanting things done my way and pushing others to conform to my view of the situation. Jealousy comes from wanting what is not mine or asking, "Why not me?" when someone else gets approval or a privilege we thought we deserved (see James 4:1-4).

Paul calls us to make no provision for the flesh and to refuse to gratify its desires. In Colossians 3:5-10, Paul says it this way:

> *Put to death therefore what is earthly in you: sexual immorality, impurity, passion, evil desire, and covetousness, which is idolatry. On account of these the wrath of God is coming. In these you too once walked, when you were living in them. But now you must put them all away: anger, wrath, malice, slander and obscene talk from your mouth. Do not lie to one another, seeing that you have put off the old self with its practices and have put on the new self, which is being renewed in knowledge after the image of its creator.*

How do we put this stuff to death? The easiest way is that we refuse to feed it. We carefully reflect on and fill our minds with the grace and treasure that is ours through the gospel as seen in early chapters of Romans. We begin to enjoy the banquet of grace and feast on it daily so that the garbage the world offers looks putrid.

Proverbs 9 drives this point home. This passage is the conclusion to an extended prologue to the rest of Proverbs, which takes the form of a letter from a father bestowing his wisdom upon his son. Throughout the prologue (and in parts of the rest of the book) wisdom is often personified as a lady. Chapter 9 serves as a summary and climax to this prologue by contrasting Lady Wisdom with Dame Folly. Verses 1-6 tell us of the life-giving feast that Lady Wisdom offers the simple among us. Verses 13-18 speak of a poisonous meal which Dame Folly seeks to seduce and bully the simple into partaking. Both would seek to have us feast at their table, but one gives life, one leads to death.

What we should find quite disturbing is that the audience of Lady Wisdom and Dame Folly are the same – the simple (verses 4 and 16). That's us, by the way. We are constantly being called by both wisdom and folly to feast at their tables.

Be careful.

> *"The Woman Folly is loud; she is seductive and knows nothing. She sits at the door of her house; she takes a seat on the highest places of the town, calling to those who pass by, who are going straight on their way, 'Whoever is simple, let him turn in here!' And to him who lacks sense she says, 'Stolen water is sweet, and bread eaten in secret is pleasant.' But he does not know that the dead are there, that her guests are in the depths of Sheol* (Proverbs 9:13-18).

Sometimes the call of folly, of sin and foolishness, is so loud that it threatens to drown out the call of wisdom, of life, joy, and peace. The call of wisdom is always there, but she will not seduce you, or deceive you. She will not raise her voice to compete with Woman Folly's screams and obnoxiousness. She will not bully you into feasting with her. She gives you the choice of feasting at her table and lets you choose. We can always choose to feast with wisdom and heeding the call that allows us to *Leave your simple ways and live, and walk in the way of insight* (9:6), whether we hear it or not.

The audience of both Lady Wisdom and Woman Folly are the same: the simple (us), but there is one slight difference. Woman Folly picks and chooses whom she will invite to her feast of death. She not only invites the simple, but the simple *who are going straight on their way* (9:15). She targets the innocent. The picture here is of a person being seduced even as they are on their way to Lady Wisdom's feast.

Be warned: ministry paints a target on your back. Not only are you going straight on your way, but you are also inviting others to follow. You are a threat to the enemy. To be in ministry means that often temptation will be stronger. Spiritual warfare will be more intense and fiercer.

We remind ourselves that our sins are leading us to a certain and terrifying appointment with the wrath of God. We remind ourselves of the grace of God that caused him to forgive us. We remind ourselves that God gave us Christ's righteousness in exchange for our sin, which he put on Christ and whom he punished in our place.

Instead of pursuing sins, we put them off and discard them like dirty clothes. In their place we are to put on the *armor of light* (Romans 13:12), which Paul also describes as putting on *the Lord Jesus Christ* (Romans 13:14).

It does not mean self-effort or that we try to imitate Christ's character or try to figure out what Jesus would have done. It does not mean trying harder and harder but failing more often. But it does mean we live in close personal fellowship with Him.

It means that Christ becomes our adornment. It means he becomes part of everything we do and everywhere we go, just like our clothing. It means that Christ becomes the core and center of our lives. It means that all we are, all we do, all we have reflects our relationship with Christ. He becomes our greatest treasure.

What do people see when they examine your life? Do they see only you or do they see a growing reflection of the Lord Jesus Christ?

Questions to Ask Ourselves

If we are to manage our households well, there are several aspects of life that must be in place. There are several questions that we need to ask ourselves. These questions will help us discover some of the issues that must be decided in our lives:

- What is my purpose in life?
- What do I want to accomplish in life?
- Which master am I going to serve?
- What will I treasure in life?
- What am I prepared to live and die for?
- How serious am I going to be about my relationship with God?
- How important is the God's Word in my life?
- How do I deal with the sin in my life?
- How am I going to train myself to be godly?
- How am I going to measure my progress toward godliness?
- What am I going to do to stand strong against the distractions and destructive current of society?
- What part will the church and community of believers play in my life?
- How am I going to invest my gifts and abilities?
- How am I going to use my earning power and the resources God has blessed me with?
- Where do other people fit into my life?

- How am I going to treat other people? Those who love me and those who oppose me.

- What am I going to do to lead other people into the life God desires for them?

- What am I doing to become the greatest husband my wife could ever have?

- What am I doing to become the greatest father my children could ever have?

The underlying question we must answer is this: Am I going to be a passive, cultural Christian who fits in with the world around me and tries to make it through life the best I can? Or am I going to be an active, biblical Christian who is prepared to stand out in the crowd and live in obedience and dependence on the Lord Jesus Christ? And do not be so arrogant as to think you can answer these questions by yourself, for yourself. Here too is where accountability is so important. Theologians often speak of a gap between our confessional theology (what we say we believe) and our functional theology (what our lives and actions tell others we believe). We know it's a scary thing to ask, but find someone close to you that cares enough to say hard things in love to you. Ask them how they see your life answering these questions.

Paul's Instructions to Timothy

As he wrote his letters to Timothy, Paul wove clear instructions into them that would help Timothy manage his own life well. In doing this he would serve as an example of godliness to the other men in the church community. He told Timothy:

- *Train yourself for godliness* (1 Tim. 4:7)

- *Set the believers an example in speech, conduct, in love, in faith, in purity* (1 Timothy 4:12).

- *Do not neglect the gift you have, which was given you by prophecy when the council of elders laid their hands on you. Practice these things, devote yourself to them, so that all may see your progress. Keep a close watch on yourself and on the teaching. Persist in this, for by so doing you will save both yourself and your hearers.* (1 Timothy 4:14-16).

- *But as for you, O man of God, flee these things* (pursuit of riches). *Pursue righteousness, godliness, faith, love, steadfastness, gentleness. Fight the good fight of the faith. Take hold of the eternal life to which you were called and about which you made the good confession in the presence of many witnesses* (1 Timothy 6:11-12).

- *Timothy, guard the deposit entrusted to you. Avoid the irreverent babble and contradictions of what is falsely called "knowledge", for by professing it some have swerved from the faith* (1 Timothy 6:20).

- *Do your best to present yourself to God as one approved, a worker who has no need to be ashamed, rightly handling the word of truth* (2 Timothy 2:15).

- *So flee youthful passions and pursue righteousness, faith, love, and peace, along with those who call on the Lord from a pure heart* (2 Timothy 2:22).

- *But as for you, continue in what you have learned and have firmly believed, knowing from whom you learned it and how from childhood you have been acquainted with the sacred writings, which are able to make you wise for salvation through faith in Christ Jesus* (2 Tim. 3:14-15).

- *As for you, always be sober-minded, endure suffering, do the work of an evangelist, fulfill your ministry* (2 Timothy 4:5).

How to Manage Yourself

What are the things that we need to do to manage ourselves well? What are the habits and practices that ought to shape the way we think, talk and act? Here are some good starting places.

Daily Time in God's Word.

In speaking of the Bible, Dane Ortlund writes, "You will stand in strength, and grow in Christ, and walk in joy, and bless this world no further than you know this book." He goes on and outlines the importance of this when he quotes the introduction to the Bibles published by the Gideons:

> The Bible contains the mind of God, the state of man, the way of salvation, the doom of sinners, and the happiness of believers. Its doctrines are holy, its precepts are binding, its histories are true, and its decisions are immutable. Read it to be wise, believe it to be safe, and practice it to be holy. It contains light to direct you, food to support you, and comfort to cheer you.
>
> It is the traveler's map, the pilgrim's staff, the pilot's compass, the soldier's sword, and the Christian's charter. Here Paradise is restored, Heaven opened, and the gates of Hell disclosed.
>
> Christ is the grand subject, our good its design, and the glory of God its end. It should fill the memory, rule the heart, and guide the feet. Read it slowly, frequently, and prayerfully. It is a mine of wealth, a paradise of glory, and a river of pleasure. It is given you in life, will be opened at the judgment, and be remembered forever.
>
> It involves the highest responsibility, rewards the greatest labor, and will condemn all who trifle with its sacred

contents.[10]

This often neglected book is the lifeline for the believer. It is the voice of God in our lives. All the words in the Bible are God's words. It is his speech; the words by which he reveals himself. Since God cannot and does not lie (Numbers 23:19; Hebrews 6:18; Titus 1:2), the Bible is fully truthful in all it says, including spiritual truth, historical details, or scientific facts (Proverbs 30:5). Because this book is truth, it is both trustworthy and authoritative. It must command our attention and call for our obedience. The Bible is also sufficient in that each of the words are God's words so that we have everything we need to be saved, to trust God, and to obey him completely. God has told us everything we need to know about his glory, our salvation, and how to live out our faith every day.[11]

Our Bible is our greatest treasure on earth, more important than our house, our money, our status, our reputation, or any of our earthly relationships. To be a man of God means this book shapes our thinking, our decision-making, our words, each of our relationships, and all our actions. For this to be true we need to dedicate significant time on a regular, and even daily basis, for reading it, meditating on it, studying it, and seeking how to follow the principles found on its pages. We should be more familiar with our Bible than with our favorite sports team, the latest movie or video game, or our financial situation. We should be more familiar with the Bible than we are with our spouses or children.

The Bible is necessary for salvation and for Christian living. It is the clear expression of God's character, his redemptive plan, and his blessing in our lives. We need to read and study the Bible

---

[10] Dane Calvin Ortlund, *Deeper: Real Change for Real Sinners*, Union (Wheaton, Illinois: Crossway, 2021), 143–144.

[11] For a more complete explanation, see Daryl Kroeker, *Gripping the Essentials: A Brief Handbook of Theology* (Surrey, BC: WorldServe Ministries, 2022), 19–27.

because it is necessary to understand the gospel. In Romans 10 Paul says,

> *For everyone who calls on the name of the Lord will be saved. How, then, can they call on him they have not believed in? And how can they believe without hearing about him? And how can they hear without a preacher? And how can they preach unless they are sent? As it is written: How beautiful are the feet of those who bring good news. But not all obeyed the gospel. For Isaiah says, Lord, who has believed our message? So faith comes from what is heard, and what is heard comes through the message about Christ* (Romans 10:13-17).

Hearing and understanding the gospel comes through the message about Christ which is found in the Bible.

We need to read and study the Bible because it is necessary for growth in the Christian life. In Matthew 4:4, Jesus quotes Deuteronomy 8:3 when he says, *It is written: Man must not live on bread alone but on every word that comes from the mouth of God.* Our spiritual life is sustained by a regular diet of God's Word. We cannot grow in our faith and trust in God unless we continually immerse ourselves in the Bible. Peter reminds us that

> *his divine power has given us everything required for life and godliness through the knowledge of him who called us by his own glory and goodness. By these he has given us very great and precious promises, so that through them you may share in the divine nature, escaping the corruption that is in the world because of evil desire* (2 Peter 1:3-4).

We need to read and study the Bible so that we will discover and know and enjoy God's will and desire for our lives. Deuteronomy 29:29 says, *The hidden things belong to the LORD our God, but the revealed things belong to us and our children forever, so that we may follow all the words of this law.* Psalm 119:1-3 tells us,

> *Blessed are those whose way is blameless, who walk in the law of the LORD! Blessed are those who keep his testimonies, who seek him*

with their whole heart, who also do no wrong, but walk in his ways!
Psalm 1 adds this picture,

> *Blessed is the man who walks not in the counsel of the wicked, nor stands in the way of sinners, nor sits in the seat of scoffers; but his delight is in the law of the LORD, and on his law he meditates day and night. He is like a tree planted by streams of water that yields its fruit in its season, and its leaf does not wither. In all that he does, he prospers.*

We are to recognize and accept the Bible as God's word (1 Thess. 2:13). We are to tremble and humble ourselves before it (Isaiah 66:2). We are to regularly enjoy them because they are sweeter than honey (Psalm 19:10; 1 Peter 2:2). Like Ezra, we are to study it carefully and obey it (Ezra 7:10; 2 Timothy 2:15). We are to preach and teach it (2 Timothy 4:2). Because the Bible is necessary for life, we need to make it our daily companion and source of spiritual food.[12]

Regular Times of Prayer

In the introduction to her book *Confessions of a Prayer Slacker*, Diane Moody asks,

> Be honest. Do you pray? I mean really pray. That shut-out-the-world, one-on-one, totally focused, praising, worshiping, talking, and listening kind of prayerful communication with your heavenly Father, who loves you and yearns to spend time with you?[13]

Great question. We all know that prayer is important for the Christian life. But most of us would have to admit that prayer, or at least, significant times of prayer, are not a regular part of our

---

[12] Ibid., 28–29.

[13] Diane Moody, *Confessions of a Prayer Slacker*, Second Edition. (OBT Bookz. Kindle Edition, 2016), Introduction.

life. With all the pressing demands of life and leadership, prayer is too often near, if not at the bottom of our list of priorities.

Why is prayer important? Because prayer is our personal response to what we know about God.[14] Prayer is the means by which we praise and worship the Lord, acknowledge his sovereign lordship over our lives, acknowledge our weaknesses and needs, ask for his provision, and claim his promises. Prayer is our act of surrender to him and the submission of our will to his. Prayer is a conversation with God based on who he is, what he says in his Word, and what he has done for us in his grace.

There are numerous outlines or plans that can be employed in our prayer times such as ACTS (Adoration, Confession, Thanksgiving, and Supplication). You can pray the Psalms or other passages of the Bible as you pray for the people in your household.[15]

There is also the pattern given by Jesus when his disciples asked him to teach them to pray. This prayer has become known as the Lord's Prayer, but it is probably better titled the Disciples' Prayer. This prayer is a wonderful outline to keep us focused during our prayer times. Here is how Tim Keller suggests it can be used:[16]

Our Father – You are a perfect, loving Father who has adopted me as your son even though I am disqualified to enter your holy and glorious presence. You are the Father who desires relationship with me and has done everything to make that relationship possible! You are the Father who knows everything about me, and yet loves me in and holds me in a grasp that will

---

[14] Timothy Keller, *Prayer: Experiencing Awe and Intimacy with God* (New York: Penguin Group, 2016), 44.

[15] A good explanation of how to do this can be found in Donald S. Whitney, *Praying the Bible* (Wheaton, Illinois: Crossway, 2015).

[16] Adapted from Keller, *Prayer*, 108–118.

never let go.

In Heaven – You are not confined to the earth and controlled by the circumstances created by human sinfulness, but you are in Heaven, above all and over all. You are the ultimate sovereign above whom there is no other; a King who created and governs a universe that is too large for me to comprehend. Yet I do not have to wait until my request climbs the ladder of rank. I can present myself and my requests at your throne, immediately, knowing the answer is final and not to be appealed to a higher court. I also know that whatever answer you give is the right answer and the best for me.

Hallowed Be Your Name – I pray that you keep me from dishonoring the name by which I am called, that you would empower me to become good and holy. I pray for a grateful heart that would be captivated by the wonder of you and your glory. I also pray that you will be glorified among the nations as believers honor God and that more and more people would honor you and call on your name.

Your Kingdom Come – Bring your kingdom into my life through the Spirit, correct my desires, and through the Word of God shape my life. I ask you Father God to extend your royal power over every part of my life – emotions, desires, thoughts, and commitments.

Your Will Be Done – I come to you with a submissive heart and mind. Keep me ready to receive what you deem best even if it might conflict with my current desires or opinion. I come ready to listen, accept and respond to you with obedience.

Give Us This Day Our Daily Bread – I come to you today for my necessities and not my excessive desires. Help me to clearly discern the difference. I ask you for the needs I face today. I want to trust that what you supply today will be enough, and that tomorrow there will be a new supply that is adequate. Help me to trust you as the giver and not trust the gifts you have given me.

Forgive Us Our Debts – I have much to confess. My sins continually pile up and each day I add to the list that would condemn me. I am thankful that because of Christ's propitiation, your wrath is satisfied and I can be forgiven over and over. I confess my sin and ask for the forgiveness Christ has earned for me.

As We Forgive Our Debtors – Give me a forgiving heart, attitude and actions. Help me to remember the vast list of offences in my life that you have graciously forgiven and help me do the same for those who have wronged me. Remove any lingering bitterness and grudges. Keep me from being a hypocrite that seeks your forgivingness but refuses to grant it to others.

Lead Us Not into Temptation – Keep me from giving in to sin. Keep me from seeking riches and power that will lead me to believe I do not need you. Keep me as well from the physical poverty and despair that will lead me to believe I cannot trust you. Guard me from being enticed away from trusting in you and toward centering my life on myself and trusting other gods.

But Deliver Us from Evil – Please protect me from the evil influences in the world around me that would call me to abandon my trust and dependence on you. Deliver me from enemies who desire to harm me.

Confession of Sin

We have already mentioned this in the previous section, but confession of sin is a vital part of progressing toward spiritual maturity. As John tells us in 1 John 1:8, we all sin. To deny that is to deceive ourselves. He goes on in 1:10 to make this very serious statement: *If we say we have not sinned, we make him a liar, and his word is not in us.* Between these two verses we find 1:9 which tells us, *If we confess our sins, he is faithful and just to forgive our sins and to cleanse us from all unrighteousness.*

Ever since Adam in the Garden in Genesis 3, people have been blaming others rather than facing their own failure and sin. It seems like we eagerly take credit for the successes in life, but we too quickly attribute failures to others. But sin is sin and there is no forgiveness or cleansing without confession and repentance. If you want to grow in your spiritual life, face your sin. Call it what it is. Agree with God that you have sinned. With those affected by your sin, agree that it was sin. As James 5:16 says, *confess your sins to one another and pray for one another, that you may be healed.* Psalm 32 reminds us, *Blessed is the one whose transgression is forgiven, whose sin is covered. Blessed is the man against whom the Lord counts no iniquity, and in whose spirit is not deceit* (Psalm 32:1-2).

How do we confess? We begin by identifying and uncovering our sin. We need to ask the Lord to show us our rebellion and defiance against His sovereign authority. We need to ask the Lord to show us all the ways we miss the mark or directly disobey His Word. We need to ask the Lord to show us the ways our twisted character has impacted and hurt others. We need to ask the Lord to show us our self-deception, and all the ways we attempt to cover and rationalize our disobedience. We need to stop calling our sin things like personality, up-bringing, culture, our opinion, or how we are wired. We need to call it what God calls it: *SIN!* We need to stop trying to cover our sin with excuses that are as flimsy as the fig leaves Adam and Eve used to cover their shame.

Many of us think we have dealt with our sin when we pray general prayers of confession – "Lord forgive me, I have sinned" – without being specific. We pray this way because we don't like our sin uncovered. We don't like our sin exposed. Too often we are like the freshman who stuffed all his dirty clothes into a sweatshirt and put the bundle in the washing machine and then the dryer. When he opened the washed bundle back in his room, he found that the clothes were still dirty. We need to untie our bundle and let God wash us clean! We need to stop covering it and stop hiding it. But agree with God that it is sin. We need to call it what God calls it!

What happens when we uncover and confess? God is faithful and just to forgive our sins. Psalm 32:5 reaffirms the result is forgiveness. This means God takes our sin away. Psalm 103:12 promises *as far as the east is from the west, so far does he remove our transgressions from us.* Confession also brings fresh security in God's love because *Many are the sorrows of the wicked, but steadfast love surrounds the one who trusts in the Lord* (Psalm 32:10). We have the ability to enter into exuberant worship and *Be glad in the Lord, and rejoice, O righteous, and shout for joy, all you upright in heart.* (Psalm 32:11). Confession will help us develop a deeper willingness to joyfully obey him.

Admission of Weaknesses

Part of our growth is to be honest with God and others about our weaknesses. This is not an easy thing for most of us. We are often taught to be strong, to try harder, to be independent. As a result, it is easy to wear a mask of strength and competence, when our reality is the opposite. It seems easier to try to do things and fix things alone than it is to ask for help from others.

I (Daryl) remember the time I got my car stuck at the bottom of an icy hill. As much as I tried, I could not get up the hill. In my stubbornness, I tried at least a dozen times to get enough speed on the dry road at the bottom so the momentum would carry me through the icy patch to the top. I failed every attempt. My exasperated wife simply said, "Call someone for help!" I obligingly called a towing company who gladly pulled my car to the top and relieved me of my money. When I later told a friend about this, he too was upset. His words were: "You should have called me! You are part of a community and in this community we admit we need help and then help each other!"

Short Account Relationships

Part of admitting our weakness is recognizing when we have done something to hurt another person and caused tension in a relationship. Part of spiritual growth is admitting our part in the tension.

Jesus told us there are two parts to this. The first is when another person has hurt us. Jesus said, *whenever you stand praying, forgive, if you have anything against anyone, so that your Father also who is in heaven may forgive you your trespasses* (Mark 11:25). The second part is when someone has something against us. In that case, Jesus said, *If your brother sins against you, go and tell him his fault, between you and him alone. If he listens to you, you have gained your brother* (Matthew 18:15). In both cases, it is up to us to initiate forgiveness and reconciliation. We don't have permission to complain that we have been wounded. We don't have permission to tell other people about the treatment we received. But we do have a command in both cases to go and make things right, to take the first step towards reconciliation, to be the one who initiates forgiveness.

Connection With a Church Community

We cannot adequately manage ourselves and grow in our Christian life without others. This is the reason the Lord put us into the body of Christ. This body is the global combination of all those who have trusted Christ's work on the cross as adequate and acceptable by God for our salvation. This global body meets in geographical locations which we call the local church. To grow we need to connect with and participate in a local community of believers.

This needs to be a place where the Word is clearly and accurately taught. It needs to be a place where worship declares the invaluable worth and glory of God. It needs to be a community where we serve and are served by the gifts given to each participant by the Holy Spirit. It needs to be a place where we are challenged to grow, supported in our struggles, disciplined in our disobedience and nurtured in our trust of God. It needs to be a place where believers are sent into the surrounding community to *proclaim the excellencies of him who called you out of darkness into his marvelous light* (1 Peter 2:9).

If we are already in church ministry leadership, we need to move past seeing the church as our place of employment. We need to see it also as the community of believers that God has placed us into so we may also continue to grow in our trust of the Lord and in the application of his Word to our lives. Be sure to find a person or people you trust that will walk with you through your personal spiritual journey. You cannot grow alone, even if you are the spiritual leader.

Physical Life

First, we need to remind ourselves that God designed our bodies and they are an amazing marvel. The Psalmist writes, *For you formed my inward parts; you knitted me together in my mother's womb. I praise you, for I am fearfully and wonderfully made* (Psalm 139:13-14).

While this is true, we also need to remind ourselves that we are not God. We have bodies that get tired, get hungry, get injured, and are impacted by disease and aging. As much as we wish we could live life as a perfectly healthy thirty-year-old, we must admit that is not going to happen.

As a result, our bodies need a significant investment. While spiritual health is a priority, we need to manage our physical health and take care of our body. Sometimes the most spiritual thing we can do is go for a brisk walk, have a sleep, or eat a good nutritious meal. John Piper writes,

> The reason people are unhealthy is because they're enslaved. They are enslaved to laziness, and they are enslaved to food. So they eat too much, and they exercise too little. And they have heart attacks and get diabetes. And God would consider that a spiritual issue.[17]

To manage yourself, you need to manage your body. How? First, sleep. God doesn't need to sleep, but we do. Sleep is a gift from God. The Psalmist writes, *It is in vain that you rise up early and go late to rest, eating the bread of anxious toil; for he gives to his beloved sleep* (Psalm 127:2). It is okay to work hard, but we need sleep to restore our energy. If we start early, work late and neglect proper rest, perhaps it is because we believe the work of God depends on us alone. We *eat the bread of anxious toil*, thinking that God needs us to do all these things for him. But Psalm 127:1 reminds us that the Lord builds the house and watches the city. We do not need to work and act as if we are the fourth person of the Trinity. God has things under control, even when we sleep.

To manage our body, we also need regular physical exercise. Paul told Timothy that even though training for godliness is the most valuable, physical training also has value (1 Timothy 4:8).

---

[17] John Piper, "How Much Does God Want Me to Care for My Physical Body?," *Desiring God*, August 7, 2009, accessed May 24, 2022, https://www.desiringgod.org/interviews/how-much-does-god-want-me-to-care-for-my-physical-body.

Some men get plenty of physical exercise in their job. But some of us have a more sedentary job where we spend a lot of time sitting in a chair. We need to get out of the chair and onto our feet. We need to regularly stretch our muscles and push our body so that we stay as healthy as possible to continue to actively serve the Lord long into our senior years.

We also need to eat carefully. Paul told the Corinthians, *So, whether you eat or drink, or whatever you do, do all to the glory of God* (1 Corinthians 10:31). While the context is about issues of conscience, this principle holds: We need to eat in a way that magnifies who God is and what he has done for us. We need to eat in a way that stewards the body God has given us.

Application Questions or Activities

1. How would you measure your spiritual discipline? Use the chart below for your evaluation.

A Disciplined Life

a. In prayer

> *... requests, prayers and intercessions be made for everyone*
> *... for kings and those in authority* (1 Tim. 2:1-2)

Weak				**Strong**
1	**2**	**3**	**4**	**5**

b. In the study of God's Word

> *... Do your best to present yourself to God as one approved*
> *... a workman who does not need to be ashamed*
> *... who handles correctly the Word of truth* (2 Tim. 2:15)
> *... have nothing to do with godless myths and old wives' tales*
> *... train yourself to be godly* (1 Tim. 4:7)

Weak				**Strong**
1	**2**	**3**	**4**	**5**

c. In living an exemplary life

> *... set an example*
> *... in speech*
> *... in life*
> *... in love*
> *... in faith*
> *... in purity* (1 Tim. 4:12)
> *... be diligent in these matters, so that everyone will see your progress* (1 Tim. 4:15)
> *... watch your life and doctrine closely* (1 Tim. 4:16)

Weak				**Strong**
1	**2**	**3**	**4**	**5**

d. In purity
   ... if a man cleanses himself
   ... he will be an instrument for noble purposes
   ... made holy
   ... useful to the Master
   ... and prepared to do any good work (2 Tim. 2:21)
   ... flee the youthful desires of youth
   ... pursue righteousness, faith, love, and peace (2 Tim. 2:22)
   ... treat ... younger women as sisters
   ... with absolute purity (1 Tim. 5:2)

Weak				**Strong**
1	2	3	4	5

2. As you review the qualities outlined above how do you measure up? Has weakness in any of these areas disqualified you from leadership at this time? Where do you need to keep growing? What do you need to do and what are you going to do to progress toward godliness in these areas?

3. Compared to the amount of time you spend entertaining yourself, how much time do you spend reading your Bible? What would you need to change to be able to spend more time in the Word? Are you prepared to make the changes? Why? Or why not?

4. In Luke 4:42 and 5:16 we discover that Jesus got up early and went to a solitary place to pray. Even though he had a schedule full of ministry responsibilities and opportunities, he often took time to get away by himself to pray. If Luke were to describe your pattern of life regarding prayer, what would he write about you? What words would best describe your

practice of prayer? (Rarely, sometimes, occasionally, here and there, often, regularly?) What decisions do you need to make and steps do you need to take to build prayer time into a regular part of your schedule?

5. Spend the next few weeks keeping track of what you pray for. You may want to consider writing out your prayers. Taking for example the previously mentioned acrostic ACTS (adoration, confession, thanksgiving, supplication), how well does the content of your prayers maintain each of those areas? For what do you pray for most? In what category do you need to spend more time?

6. How often do you confess sin? How much time usually goes by between the moment you've sinned and the moment you admit it was sin? What happens when you refuse or put off confessing your sin (see Psalm 32:1-5)? How is your confession of sin tied to maintaining a regular Bible reading and prayer time?

7. When was the last time you humbled yourself and asked someone for help? What would have happened if you had asked for help? What happened because you did not ask for help? Why was it so hard to humble yourself? What did you learn from the experience?

8. Are there any people from the past or in the present whom you need to have a conversation about making things right? Make a list. Pray for those people and make a commitment to go and have those conversations.

9. Are you connected to a church where you joyfully participate in the life and ministry of the community? If not, why not? What does your lack of participation say about your commitment to the Lord Jesus?

10. How is your physical health? Are there things you need to do different that will improve your health and help you better glorify God?

Chapter 2: You and Your Wife

1 Timothy 3:4 tells us an elder *must manage his own household well.* In the original language of the New Testament (Greek) *household* is the word *oikos.* This word is used to refer to those who are living within your home and are under your leadership and influence. In the New Testament it included one's wife and children. It included household employees or servants. In some cases, it even included business partners and other associates that were impacted by the leadership of the household. Today, this term may represent something different in various cultures. But we do know it certainly includes the relationship a man is to have with his wife.

The subject of marriage can be a very difficult topic. Part of the difficulty comes from our sinful nature which does not like what the Bible says. It is contrary to what we naturally like or desire to do. What the Bible says about marriage conflicts with the cultural norms that seek to govern our society and the worldview of its members. At this point we need to decide whether we believe the Bible gives us suggestions from God on how to live, or whether the Bible is the inspired, authoritative, sufficient Word of God. Is this book what God has called us to do and to live by, or is it a collection of stories and ideas that really do not matter?

Do we allow the Bible to speak to us, to challenge and reshape our thinking, and to guide our behavior? Or is it only an opinion or idea that we can take or leave, depending on how we feel or how the world around us thinks?

We personally believe the Bible is the inspired, authoritative, inerrant, sufficient Word of God. It is the very breath of God that we must listen to, that we must obey, and we must allow it to change our lives (2 Tim. 3:16-17). We believe that, from Genesis

1:1 to Revelation 22:21, *everything* in Scripture was written for God's glory and our good. We obey because it's right and righteous to do so. We obey because we trust that it is good for us even if it doesn't feel like it. We obey because our very lives, both eternal and mortal, depend on it. With that in mind, let's see what the Bible says about our marriages.

Finding a Wife

We often think of marriage in terms of the woman we will marry. But it is more about who we are as men when we get married. We need to look at ourselves and ask if we are the kind of man a woman wants to marry. Would she see and know that we are her gift from the Lord? This question is not about how we look, how much we have or what we do for a living. This question is about our character. Are we tender? Are we kind? Are we forgiving? Are we a willing servant of others? Do we care how people around us feel? Are we willing to be inconvenienced when others need help? Are we a giver or a taker? Do we love ourselves more than we love the Lord? Is our entertainment more important to us than time with the Lord? Are we more about power or position than holiness? Are we the kind of man that a woman would joyfully follow, knowing that she would be safe and loved? Finding a wife is not just about the woman, but about examining who we are and looking carefully at what we bring into the relationship.

Proverbs 18:22 puts it well: *He who finds a wife finds a good thing and obtains favor from the Lord.* One of the greatest gifts God has ever given me (Daryl) has been Tamara. The Lord brought Tamara into my life shortly after my first wife was killed in an automobile crash. She was the perfect gift from God who helped me through my grief and has walked with me now through 40+

years of marriage, family and ministry leadership.

And I (Richard) echo this when I think of my wife, Melissa. She and I often joke that we've been married for 27 years; happily married for 22. I must confess, to call the first five years of our marriage difficult is a gross understatement. She was physically ill with what was a relatively minor but difficult to diagnose chronic disorder, which, also affected her mood. However I was totally unprepared to be the husband she needed as I was incredibly immature. In addition, I was nurturing a pervasive sin pattern that I wouldn't find victory over until five years after the wedding. Melissa taught me what forgiveness looks like. She demonstrated the gospel in such a way that I now can teach it and have some degree of confidence that I know what it looks like – because I've seen it in how Melissa forgave and showed grace to me.

What does the Bible say about a wife? Here is a sample:

1) She is a gift from God (Prov. 18:22; 19:14). Prov. 19:14 says, *House and wealth are inherited from fathers, but a prudent wife is from the Lord.*

2) She is your partner in life …*they are heirs with you of the grace of life* (1 Peter 3:7). She shares an equal destiny, and you have the privilege of walking together toward the gates of heaven.

3) She is to be your only lover. *Let your fountain be blessed, and rejoice with the wife of our youth, a lovely deer, a graceful doe. Let her breasts fill you at all times with delight; be intoxicated always in her love. Why should you be intoxicated, my son, with a forbidden woman and embrace the bosom of an adulteress?* (Proverbs 5:18-20).

Earlier we noted from Genesis 2:18-23, that loneliness was a God-sized problem requiring a God-sized solution, which came in the form of Eve, Adam's wife. If you continue in that passage, verse 24 says: *"Therefore a man shall leave his father and his mother and hold fast to his wife, and they shall become one flesh."* It seems that "becoming one flesh" is a climax of the passage. It is meant to be a God-sized celebration to the God-sized solution, given to solve mankind's God-sized problem of loneliness.

To put it more grandly (and even more accurately), sex was given to us by God, as a totally unique form of worship, to be used ONLY in the context of praising Him specifically for solving our problem of loneliness. And yes, it is a celebration. It is meant to *feel* like a celebration.

To drive the point home further, God tells us in Genesis 2:25 *"And the man and his wife were both naked and not ashamed."* There is but one place on earth that we see people "naked and unashamed," that being the Garden of Eden, prior to the fall. Sex with our spouses is meant to be a glimpse of what it was like before we brought shame into the world by sinning in Genesis 3. Further, sex with our spouses is the only place we should be totally free from the shame of our sin and regret, which means it's a foreshadowing of what heaven will feel like. To understand this is to further enhance our worship through physical intimacy. In short, sex is meant to be used as worship, thanking the God who is good enough and powerful enough to solve the world's most profound problem: loneliness. This means that sex for our own gratification is a perversion.

Physical relationships with multiple partners (even if they come and go one at a time), extramarital affairs, homosexuality, gender fluidity, etc. are all in essence self-worship. They celebrate what the individual wants and needs, or what culture says the individual should want or need. This passage tells us that sex is not about fulfilling our "needs." It's about loving our spouses in the context of loving our God. The fact that it's an awesome experience is simply a blessed gift from its creator.

4) She is to be your helper. *Then the Lord God said, "It is not good that the man should be alone, I will make a helper fit for him."* (Genesis 2:18). *Helper* means one who supplies strength in the area that is lacking in the one being helped. She provides strength in the areas where you are weak.

Helper does not mean that she is your servant or slave to do whatever you demand of her. To sharpen our understanding of this, the Bible uses the word *helper* in several ways. It is used of God who helped deliver Moses from the sword of Pharoah (Exodus 18:4). It is used to describe him as the one *who rides through the heavens to your help, through the skies in majesty* and the *shield of your help* (Deuteronomy 33:26, 29). In Psalm 70:5, the Psalmist writes, *But I am poor and needy; hasten to me, O God! You are my help and my deliverer; O Lord, do not delay.* Psalm 121:1-2 adds, *I lift up my eyes to the hills. From where does my help come? My help comes from the Lord, who made heaven and earth.* This word also describes the work of the Holy Spirit who is given to us by God. Jesus said, *And I will ask the Father, and he will give you another Helper, to be with you forever, even the Spirit of truth, whom the world cannot receive, because it neither sees him nor knows him. You know him, for he dwells with you and will be in you* (John 14:16-17). The help of our wives is not a demeaning role, but one that is necessary and powerful. A helper is an extraordinary gift from God.

5) She is your sister in the Lord. *For as many of you as were baptized into Christ have put on Christ. There is neither Jew nor Greek, there is neither slave nor free, there is no male and female, for you are all one in Christ Jesus* (Galatians 3:27-28). The Bible teaches that while we may have different roles within the family and the church, we are equal in Christ. There is no distinction in our redemption but all are equally redeemed, forgiven and have become members of the body of Christ. Your wife is your sister in the Lord.

If these things describe a wife, how does the Bible describe a good wife?

- She is a woman of godly character. *An excellent wife is the crown of her husband, but she who brings shame is like rottenness in his bones.* (Proverbs 12:4). *Charm is deceitful, and beauty is vain, but a woman who fears the Lord is to be praised.* (Proverbs 31:30)

- She is a woman who is careful and not rash. She is described as *a prudent wife* (Proverbs 19:14) Prudent means one who is careful. She thinks things through. She is thoughtful and does not make sudden or reactionary decisions.

- She is a woman who is not self-centered but who takes her responsibilities seriously (Proverbs 31:10-28).

If you are single and you want to find a good wife, it begins with you. You need to be a good man. Be a godly man. Be a man who serves others first. Be a man who takes his responsibilities and assignments seriously. Be a man who looks beyond physical appearances (1 Samuel 16:7).

Here are some of the questions you should ask when

considering a marriage to a particular woman:[18]

- What does she believe about God, about the Bible, about Christ, about redemption, about eternal life?

- Who does she worship? How does she worship? How important is worship to her? What part does church ministry play in her life?

- What are her regular practices regarding reading the Bible and spending time in prayer?

- What does she believe about marriage? What does she believe about leadership and submission in marriage? How does she see household tasks being shared? How does she understand who initiates sex and how often?

- What does she believe about family? How many children does she want to have? What are the appropriate ways to discipline children?

- What are her goals in life? What are her dreams?

- What does she believe about money? How will you make decisions about money and purchases?

- What does she believe about work? Should she work outside the home? What are her views on having others look after the children? What will determine where you live?

- What makes her angry? What does she do with her anger? How does she handle conflict with others?

- Are there any sicknesses or physical problems that could impact the marriage? Are there any habits that will adversely affect health?

There are some cautions to consider when finding the answers

---

[18] Adapted from John Piper, "Topics for Conversation When a Man and a Woman Are Considering Marriage," *Desiring God*, January 1, 1995, accessed May 24, 2022, https://www.desiringgod.org/articles/topics-for-conversation-when-a-man-and-a-woman-are-considering-marriage.

to these kinds of questions. First, you cannot ask them unless you are prepared to answer them. Second, do not make them a checklist to be covered in one or two meetings. Instead use them to get to know her and her thoughts over time. Third, no one is perfect. Are you willing to live with what you perceive as an imperfection or something you cannot fully agree upon?

Marrying a Wife

In Genesis 2 we learn that the marriage relationship was instituted by God as part of his creation work. He created Adam in his likeness and put in him the Garden of Eden with instructions to work it and look after it. It is not clear how much time intervened between Adam's creation and God's comment that it was not good for him to be alone. Perhaps it was long enough for Adam to see that every one of the animals had a partner except him. Perhaps it was long enough for him to feel alone.

Since it was not good for him to be alone, God made a companion, a helper that corresponded to him who was also made in God's likeness. He put Adam into a deep sleep and then took one of his ribs and made a woman from it. When Adam awoke, God brought the woman to him. When he saw her, he fell in love at first sight and sang a poetic song. His response was, "Wow! She is incredible!"

The explanation of this new partnership is given in Genesis 2:24-25, *Therefore a man shall leave his father and his mother and hold fast to his wife, and they shall become one flesh. And the man and his wife were both naked and were not ashamed.* This new relationship was transparent and without shame. The two became one and began the journey through life together.

It would be nice if we read that they lived happily ever after.

But that is not where the story takes us. The two eventually rebelled against God and ate of the fruit of the tree he had forbidden. This not only changed their relationship with God, but it also had an impact on their relationship with each other. From this point forward, each day of this marriage – and every subsequent marriage – would bring the potential of happiness and life or conflict and brokenness.

As we consider marriage, we need to recognize that marriage is not a sacrament or a means for a couple to obtain special grace from God. Nor is it a conditional contract that is formed and maintained and later dissolved by two individuals. It is not a business arrangement or a deal where one stays committed if they feel good or if the other meets their needs and keeps them happy.

Marriage is a covenant. It is a sacred bond between husband and wife and between the couple and God. To understand this, we need to look again at the very first marriage as it is described in Genesis 2:21-24.

> *So the Lord God caused a deep sleep to fall upon the man, and while he slept took one of his ribs and closed up its place with flesh. And the rib that the Lord God had taken from the man he made into a woman and brought her to the man. Then the man said, "This is at last bone of my bones and flesh of my flesh; she shall be called Woman, because she was taken out of Man." Therefore a man shall leave his father and his mother and hold fast to his wife, and they shall become one flesh.*

From this first marriage we see that woman is fashioned from man – therefore they are one. They are made of the same material. One is not better than the other.

God made only one woman, therefore His plan for marriage was heterosexual monogamy. All other forms of marriage are outside of God's design.

Marriage is to be a priority. Man is to leave his father and mother indicating his obligation to his wife overrides even his duty to his parents. And yes, this includes your ministry. Your family takes precedence over your church ministry.

Marriage demands faithfulness. The man is to *hold fast* to his wife. There are to be no others. Malachi 2:14 describes a wife as *your companion and your wife by covenant.*

Marriage as a covenant means that the couple commits themselves to the following:

- Marriage is Permanent – It is a relationship established by God (Matthew 19:6; Mark 10:9).

- Marriage is Sacred – It is a relationship before and under God (Genesis 2:22).

- Marriage is Intimate – It is a relationship that unites a man and woman in a "one flesh" bond (Genesis 2:23-25). It includes leaving parents to form a new kinship relationship between previously unrelated individuals.

- Marriage is Mutual – It is a relationship of free self-giving between a man and a woman. It is a relationship of giving and not getting (Ephesians 5:25-30). Too many get married for sexual satisfaction, or a beautiful object to make them feel good or for the privilege of being looked after. No, we get married so we can give!

- Marriage is Exclusive – It is a relationship where no other individuals are allowed to interfere with the commitment to each other (Genesis 2:22-25; 1 Corinthians 7:2-5).

Loving a Wife

Men, once you are married, you are commanded by God to love your wife. Ephesians 5 makes this very clear.

Husbands, love your wives, as Christ loved the church and gave himself up for her, that he might sanctify her, having cleansed her by the washing of water with the word, so that he might present the church to himself in splendor, without spot or wrinkle or any such thing, that she might be holy and without blemish. In the same way husbands should love their wives as their own bodies. He who loves his wife loves himself. For no one ever hated his own flesh, but nourishes and cherishes it, just as Christ does the church, because we are members of his body. "Therefore a man shall leave his father and mother and hold fast to his wife, and the two shall become one flesh." This mystery is profound, and I am saying that it refers to Christ and the church. However, let each one of you love his wife as himself, and let the wife see that she respects her husband.

Did you notice how many times the word *love* or *loved* or *loves* is used in these verses? These words appear six times. This is the central theme or focus of Paul's message to husbands.

What kind of love is Paul taking about? He is talking about *agape* love, the kind of love that sacrifices for the other person. This love is an ongoing love. It is love that is not deserved or based on merit. It means a husband is to love his wife even when she seems undeserving or unloving. This means the husband is to love unconditionally. It means he is to seek her highest good. It means his love is not dependent on her response. It means his love is not governed by emotion but is an act of the will. It means he is to love his own wife and not someone else's wife.

How are we to love our wives? *As Christ loved the church* (5:25), and *as their own bodies* (5:28). How did Christ love the church? He gave himself up for the church. Christ took the initiative in handing himself over to death. He went to the cross as a willing victim. This demonstration was the supreme display of love for those he would call to be his bride.

Christ also *sanctified* the church or chose her to be set aside in a permanent relationship (5:26). Christ chose the church for a special and exclusive relationship.

Christ also *cleansed* the church from her sin *by the washing of water with the word* (5:26). He took all that would keep her from that special relationship and sacrificed himself so that she would be beautiful. As a result, he will *present the church to himself without spot or wrinkle or any such thing, that she might be holy and without blemish* (5:27). He sees the church as his gift and will display her as a treasure of his grace for all eternity. The church is pictured as a beautiful young bride whose garments are spotless and unwrinkled.

The husband is also to love his wife as his own body (5:28). How is this done? He *nourishes* it. He cares for it physically. He also *cherishes* it. He cares for it emotionally. The husband and wife are one body, and the husband should provide the physical and emotional support she needs. Since becoming one flesh she is his body.

But there is one more thing. Paul quotes Genesis 2:24 where it says *Therefore a man shall leave his father and mother and hold fast to his wife, and the two shall become one flesh* (5:31). This quote summarized the reason for a husband loving his wife as himself, but it also points out another important point regarding how a man is to love his wife. The husband moves from a relationship of dependency and guidance under his parents to a new life of partnership with his wife. As one body, they are to walk through and work through the issues of life together.

What are the implications of all this? How is a husband to love his wife? How are you to love your wife? How am I to love my wife?

Give yourself totally and sacrificially to loving her (5:25). This includes all your self-interests and desires and goes as far as the ultimate sacrifice of life itself.

Treat her as someone special (5:26). Recognize the exclusiveness of the relationship which is not to be shared with or replaced by anyone or anything else.

See her as the beautiful person God created her to be (5:27). Be an active part in helping her grow to be more and more like Christ, not by being a preacher, but by loving her and modeling for her what it means to grow in Christlikeness.

Take care of her physically and emotionally and in so doing you will be taking care of yourself (28-30).

Live with her as a co-partner in the decisions of life (5:31). Live life together, depending on each other's unique perspective, wisdom and giftedness.

Why should you love your wife? The answer is found in Ephesians 5:32 where Paul writes, *This mystery is profound, and I am saying that it refers to Christ and the church.* It seems that Paul is saying that God instituted marriage because the church is Christ's body.

This means that the joining of husband and wife as one flesh was originally intended to be a living picture of the union Christ has with the church. Your marriage is a picture of the love of Christ and the oneness of Christ and his bride, the church.

Ephesians 3:10 tells us the purpose of the church is *that through the church the manifold wisdom of God might now be made known to the rulers and authorities in the heavenly places.* One of the ways to display the manifold wisdom of God or to declare the glorious grace of God, is through our marriage. If you want people to see a living demonstration of his love, grace and care for the church, one of the best places to see it is in a Christian marriage. By the way, this is one of the reasons so many Christian marriages are under attack. If Satan can destroy the practical picture he can undermine the wonderful truths of God's grace.

Biblical love is a decision that brings security to a relationship. If love for your wife is only a feeling, you will fall in and out of love depending on all sorts of things, including the weather. But when it is a decision, it brings security to the relationship.

Serving a Wife

Besides sacrificially loving your wife, how can you serve her? The Bible suggests several things. First, you must leave your dependance on your parents (Ephesians 5:31). This is not necessarily a geographical leaving but certainly leaving behind your dependence on them. Don't let them be the first place you go for advice and direction. Have those conversations with your wife first. If you need outside counsel in decision-making, you can talk to your parents, just don't make them the first ones in the decision-making process.

Second, do not be harsh with your wife (Colossians 3:19). There was a tendency in the Roman world of the New Testament for men to rage bitterly against their wives and mistreat them. Because of their greater strength and louder voices, men in their sinful natures are prone to use harsh words, threats, unkindness and even physical violence to intimidate their wives. In one culture where I (Daryl) shared this message with pastoral leaders, one of them asked: "Is it okay for a pastor to beat his wife if she does not submit?" I was dumbfounded by the question and gasped a prayer for wisdom. The Lord then directed me to ask the wives who were present: "Ladies, when your husband beats you, does it help you submit?" The room was deathly quiet for a minute, but I continued to wait. Finally, one lady in the back of the room stood up and said, "No, it doesn't help."

Harshness, oppression and abuse are about control, and they are not only physical. Anything used to get your way and establish dominance over another should be considered abuse. Biblically the word abuse is synonymous with oppression. Hear the heart of Jesus on this subject: *The Spirit of the Lord is upon me, because he has anointed me to proclaim good news to the poor. He has sent me to proclaim liberty to the captives and recovering of sight to the blind, to set at liberty those who are oppressed, to proclaim the year of the Lord's favor* (Luke 4:18-19). Some translations use the word *downtrodden* instead of *oppressed.* But whichever word is used, the Lord hates oppression. Yes, this passage is explicitly referring to spiritual oppression, but in revealing his God-appointed mission to free His people from their oppressive beliefs, practices and leadership, Jesus is revealing his heart. He hates all forms of oppression. He sees the victim and cries with her, comforts her, will visit vengeance upon her perpetrator (see Heb. 10:26-31).

In her book about abuse, Darby Strickland defines these five different categories of abuse: physical, sexual, emotional, spiritual, and financial abuse.[19] It is astonishing how few men — even pastors — recognize abuse as anything other than physical, and consider themselves innocent of abuse and oppression because they've never hit a woman. But make no mistake. Demanding that your wife perform sexual acts that she's not comfortable with, consistently demeaning and devaluing her as a person, using religion to guilt or shame her into doing something she would otherwise be unwilling to do, or micromanaging the finances in such a way that gets you what you want at the expense of your wife's and family's needs and desires, are all just as legitimately defined as abuse as is beating your wife.[20]

---

[19] Darby Strickland, Is it Abuse: A Biblical Guide to Identifying Domestic Abuse and Helping Victims, (2020: Phillipsburg, NJ, P&R Publishing).

[20] Just to be clear, each of these examples are but one example of each of the five types of abuse. Sexual abuse, for example, may also include things like using sex as a bargaining chip to get what you want (again, this is but another example).

Pastors and church leaders are perhaps most susceptible to the category of spiritual abuse. One of the most extreme examples is of a pastor some years ago who demanded that his wife go to strip clubs with him, because Ephesians 5:22 says *Wives, submit to your husbands.* Granted, most instances of spiritual oppression are far more subtle, which in some senses makes it far more damaging.

As men who are charged with leading the church, we can use what we have learned in our theological studies to dominate and not to serve our family and our church community. It is so easy to subtly warp the truths of Scripture to justify our offenses against another person. Some leaders use principles of biblical stewardship to justify a refusal to let their wives buy some much needed shoes, even as they buy themselves a very expensive tool or toy. Some use the biblical principles of male leadership to justify making significant decisions without informing their wives or telling them but ignoring their valid objections. Others turn God's call for a wife to respect her husband into a demand their wives spend little or no time with their friends, because their responsibility is only to the husband, the family, and the house. Some even use the biblical principle of submission to force their wives into the role domestic servants, or more accurately, slaves.

Abusers choose to justify and shift blame rather than repent. They seem to be incapable of recognizing that they did anything wrong. This often comes out in the form of what clinicians have come to refer to as "gas lighting". The term is derived from a 1938 play, "The Gas Light" which was made into a film in 1944.[21] This is the story of a husband who commits himself to driving his wife insane. He does it gradually, over a period of months by reducing the brightness of the gas-fed lights by reducing gas flow to

---

[21] Patrick Hamilton, *Gas Light,* ed. David Jacklin, (2014: Balderson, ON, Barndoor Productions).

convince her she's going blind. As he does this, he tells her it's all her fault she can't see anymore. This is why the term "gaslighting" is an accurate label given to a husband who is oppressing his wife but blaming her for his abuse.

Gaslighting takes so many forms that it's hard to come up with examples that illustrates its scope, but it may look something like this:

- "I wouldn't have to watch pornography or step outside the marriage if you'd just be freer with your body and more adventurous in the bedroom." After all, Paul commands a wife give to her husband his conjugal rights (1 Cor. 7:3).

- "I know I shouldn't have hit you but if you had supper on the table like I asked you to, I wouldn't have had to hit you."

- "I work so hard! It's not too much to ask that the house is clean when I get home. If you had just done what I asked, I wouldn't have lost my temper."

- "You don't know enough about our finances to have an opinion as to whether or not we should buy that boat."

- "You aren't smart enough to help make the decisions in this house."

In other words, the abuser's reality is shaped by denial and blame shifting. As these examples indicate, gaslighting often has to do with the unrealistic, unwarranted, and selfish (often to the point of being narcissistic) expectations on the part of the oppressor far more than it does on his wife's sinfulness. But even if your wife does require legitimate confrontation or gentle reproof, it is no excuse for your sinful response. There is no cause-and-effect relationship between your sin and hers. In other words, no matter how bad your wife sins against you, you are still responsible to God and your wife for your sinful response. Your response to her can and should always be speaking the truth in love (Eph. 4:15). And when you fail to respond in that manner, your next step *must* be repentance. To respond in any other way is to forfeit your right to confront her in her sin.

There is no room for even a hint of oppression and abuse in the Christian marriage. Instead, we are called to love our wives as Christ tenderly loves the Church. Romans 12:16-21 exhorts us to respond to wrongs done to us with good. When our spouses wrong us, we are called to repay with good. We are called to act righteously even in the face of offence. Paul tells us in this passage that our righteous and good response to another's offence against us invites them unto repentance. In verse 20 Paul writes, *if your enemy is hungry, feed him; if he is thirsty, give him something to drink; for by so doing you will heap burning coals on his head.* The common interpretation of this verse says that heaping burning coals on his head is to shame your enemy into repentance and restitution. But this doesn't fit with the context of the verse which teaches us how we are to treat our enemies. Here in Romans 12, Paul is quoting Proverbs 25:21-22, which seems to have been borrowed from Egyptian wisdom literature. In Egyptian folklore contemporary to the time of Proverbs 25, is the story of a man who greatly offended another who was hosting a party. As an act of repentance, the offender showed up at the party with a tray of hot coals on his head, in essence saying, "I will bear the level of pain that I have caused you." There is strong evidence that this story initiated a common repentance ritual in Egyptian and ancient near-eastern culture. Whether Paul was aware of this ritual by the time he writes the book of Romans is doubtful, but by the time of Paul's ministry, "heaping burning coals on your enemy's head had become a well-established idiomatic expression referring to repentance; not penance or manipulation of your enemy into restitution, but genuine repentance."[22]

Third, to serve our wives, we need to be understanding. Peter wrote, *Likewise, husbands, live with your wives in an understanding way, showing honor to the woman as the weaker vessel, since they are heirs with you of the grace of life, so that your prayers may not be hindered* (1 Peter 3:7). We need to honor her, which means to always speak well of her. This also means we do not demand that she be submissive to us. We need to protect her. She is physically weaker and often more vulnerable, and we need to go out of our way to make sure she is safe. We need to respect her as our partner in life. God has put us together so that we might experience life and grace together. You are not better than her and need to walk hand-in-hand with her through life.

Did you notice why we need to serve our wife? *So that your prayers may not be hindered.* Our prayers are hindered, our sermons are hollow, and our leadership undermined, if we are disobedient in this area of our life.

Leading a Wife

Many husbands around the world think that leading their wife is done by giving rules and commands. They take a power position and demand that their wife submit and obey. They treat their wives as though they were servants or slaves. But is that the picture the Bible gives us?

Ephesians 5:23 tells us, *For the husband is head of the wife even as Christ is the head of the church, his body, and is himself its Savior.* As the

---

[22] William Klassen, *Coals of Fire: Sign of Repentance or Revenge.* New Testament Studies, Volume 9, Issue 4, July 1963, (Oxford, Cambridge University Press) pp. 337-350. Published online, (2009, Oxford, Cambridge University Press). Klassen's conclusions are dependent in part on the work of Egyptologist Siegfried Morenz, first published in: F.L. Griffith, *Stories of the High Priests of Memphis (1900: Oxford, Cambridge University Press).*

covenant head, Jesus went to the cross and shed his blood for you and all your sins. The result is that you have a new relationship of grace.

As a husband, you are the covenant head of your family. Some foolish men sinfully misrepresent and misapply the headship principle. They use it as an opportunity to rule over their wives, to demand obedience and submission, to treat them as inferior to themselves. But just as Jesus leads through suffering, we too are called to lead through suffering. That means we lead our wives through humble service, love, care, protection and provision. Just as the Lord Jesus our Head leads us.

Listen to Titus 2:2. *Older men are to be sober-minded, dignified, self-controlled, sound in faith, in love and in steadfastness.* Titus 2:6-8 adds, *Likewise, urge the younger men to be self-controlled. Show yourself in all respects to be a model of good works, and in your teaching show integrity, dignity, and sound speech that cannot be condemned.*

How do we lead our wife? Through our godly example. Through our tender love. We lead through publicly treasuring her and honoring her with your words to her and about her. We lead through our study and application of God's Word – not just for others, but for our own life. We lead through our prayer life. But don't pray that she will change, instead, pray that God would make you the best possible husband she could ever have. We lead through the investment of time. She is our priority commitment. Spend time together each day, each week, each month, each year.

We lead through a servant heart. We meet her needs in practical ways without being asked. We lead through our communication. Talk to her and let her talk to you. Listen to her without trying to solve her problems. Women want to be heard but they don't always want their husband to fix their problem. They want an ear, not a solution.

We lead through our protection. Don't let your ministry work eat up your marriage by it becoming a mistress that feeds your need for self-worth. Don't let your self-worth be determined by what you do in the ministry but let it be by who you are in Christ Jesus.

One last comment about leadership: Leadership is far more about responsibility than it is about authority. In other words, as the head of the household, men will be held more responsible by God for the spiritual and relational health of the marriage than will their wife. It is an awesome responsibility, requiring nothing less than the power of the Holy Spirit to help them fulfill that responsibility.

Ministering With a Wife

If you are involved in the ministry of the church or an organization, how do you minister with your wife?

First, recognize that your wife is not you and will not respond to situations, needs and issues the same way you will. She will have her own perspective and she will respond according to the gifts and abilities God has given her. Don't argue about whose viewpoint is correct or whose side of the counseling situation is right. Listen to each other. God will often use your wife to give you a clearer picture of the situation you might be facing.

Let your wife develop her interests and use her own gifts and abilities. She may not meet the expectation you or the church family have for her. Not every pastor's wife is a speaker, counselor, or confident musician. Let your wife pursue the ministry that best suits her gifts and abilities and passions. Don't squeeze her into your mold. In my early days of ministry, while applying for youth pastorates, I (Richard) was turned down by a church that was otherwise very interested because I told them that my wife would prefer to volunteer in the children's ministry rather than work with me in the youth ministry. Both authors have witnessed churches that have put undue burdens on the wives of pastors simply because they were the pastor's wife. Most pastor's wives are no more or no less called to serve than the normal layman. Do not allow your ministry to place undue weight on her shoulders.

Protect her from unwarranted and untrue criticism. She needs to know that you are her supporter, friend and confidant. Your covenant relationship with her supersedes your ministry relationships.

Do not try to be her pastor, teacher, or counselor. Be her husband. She will learn from you, but let that learning come from how you love her and not how you try to formally instruct her.

Last and very important, do not sacrifice her and your relationship with her for the sake of the ministry you might be involved in. The Lord has given her to you to love, care for, protect, nurture, and support on his behalf. Make her your priority and let her know through your time management decisions that she is your priority. When you say you will do something for her or with her, do it when you said you would. Barring an absolute emergency, don't let your ministry activity override your commitment to your wife.

My wife and I (Richard) have found over the years that so often life and ministry get in the way of this. It may not seem very romantic to plan things like vacations, date night and pillow talk ahead of time, but we have found it necessary. We plan time away each year – often several times a year – just to refocus our attention on each other. We faithfully have date night at least every other week. With but very few exceptions we set aside time to talk with each other daily, either at meals and/or at bedtime. The work of ministry is never finished. Life will always demand all your attention. If you don't fervently and stubbornly protect your time with your family, the busyness of ministry and life will always creep in and take over.

So, brothers, how do we manage our household well? We begin with ourselves. We allow the Lord Jesus Christ to be our Lord every day. Then, through our growing relationship with the Lord, we give godly, loving, tender, sacrificial leadership to our wife just as Christ did for us and for His church.

Application Questions or Activities

1. How would you measure the heart and health of your home? Use the chart below for your evaluation.

A Loving Heart

a. One who is gentle.

> ... *not violent but gentle* (1 Tim. 3:3)
>
> ... *not lording it over those entrusted to you* (1 Peter 5:3)

An elder must not be the kind of person who strikes back with a blow when they are offended or annoyed. He must be considerate of the feelings others, refusing to insist on his own rights or demands. He must be able to make room for others who think and live differently than he.

Weak				Strong
1	2	3	4	5

b. One who has an open home and hand.

> ... *hospitable* (1 Tim. 3:2)
>
> ... *he must be hospitable* (Titus 1:8)

An elder must be a lover of strangers. He must be a people person, someone who can make others feel comfortable and at home. He must have time for people and have an open home as evidence.

Weak				Strong
1	2	3	4	5

c. One who cares for the needs of others.

> ... *be shepherds of God's flock that is under your care* (1 Peter 5:2)
>
> ... *be shepherds of the church of God, which he bought with his own blood* (Acts 20:28)

An elder must view his responsibility as primarily that of a care giver and not solely as an administrative executive.

Weak				Strong
1	2	3	4	5

A Healthy Home

a. One who is faithful to his wife.

> ... *the husband of but one wife* (Titus 1:6)
>
> ... *the husband of but one wife* (1 Tim. 3:2)

Bible scholars differ on the meaning of this phrase. Some say it means an elder must be married. Some suggest an elder can be married only once during his lifetime. Others say it means an elder must be married to only one woman at a time. Whatever the accepted interpretation, an elder must at least be a one-woman kind of man. He must be totally devoted to his wife. He must not be flirtatious nor accused regarding any relationships with other women.

Weak				Strong
1	2	3	4	5

b. One whose wife is living a godly life.

> ... *women worthy of respect*
>
> ... *not malicious talkers*
>
> ... *but temperate*
>
> ... *and trustworthy in everything* (1 Tim. 3:11).

Weak				Strong
1	2	3	4	5

2. As you review the qualities outlined above how do you measure up? Has weakness in any of these areas disqualified you from leadership at this time? Where do you need to keep growing? What do you need to do and what are you going to do to progress toward godliness in these areas?

3. If you are single, think through our explanation of what a good wife should look like at the beginning of this chapter. In what ways are your expectations of your future bride in line with the biblical description of a good wife? What are you looking for in a wife that may not line up with Scripture?

4. What is your definition of submission? How does your definition agree with the Bible's definition? How does the Bible challenge it?

5. Where are you falling short in your responsibilities as a husband? For what do you need to repent of to your spouse and to God? Are there any abusive behaviors that need to be addressed and repented of?

6. What have you done this past week to intentionally serve your wife? What are you planning to do in the coming week? Be specific and make a plan to follow through.

7. What practices have you put in place to protect your time with your spouse and family, to keeps life and ministry from encroaching upon it? What practices do you *need* to put in place?

Chapter 3: You and Your Children

Before the ages began, you were called to salvation (Ephesians 1:4). That means it rests on no merit of your own. It rests on no work of your manufacture. It rests only on the sovereign will of God because of his own purpose and grace.

Before the ages began you were called to ministry (Ephesians 2:10). That means it rests not on your ability, wisdom, power, education, influence or charisma. It rests only on the sovereign will of God because of his own purpose and grace.

Each morning when we get up, we ought to celebrate that we are saved by grace, called by grace, are kept by grace, and are called to the ministry of grace! We need to rest in the fact that God has called us and planned for us and will provide for us. Our response to his call to salvation and ministry must result in a life of worship, obedience and service. When we grasp the greatness of his grace and our own complete unworthiness for salvation or ministry leadership, we can only fall on our faces and worship with awe and wonder. Our only option is to respond to him in obedience and service.

A very important area of obedience and service is in relation to our families. It is through the good management of our homes that we can be identified as qualified to give leadership to the church family.

As we continue our study on how to manage our households, we return to 1 Timothy 3:4 where we read, he *must manage his own household well, with all dignity keeping his children submissive.*

The relationship between a father and his children is woven through the pages of Scripture. For God declares himself to be the wonderful Heavenly Father who provides for, who loves, teaches, disciplines, and tenderly leads his children.

Jesus gave us a wonderful picture of our Father in Heaven when he told the parable of the prodigal son who left the security of home to find his own way in the world. Even as the son drifted further and further from the desires of his father, it was his father who waited on the road every day hoping and praying and waiting for his son to return.

Psalm 127:3 tells us, *Behold, children are a heritage from the Lord, the fruit of the womb a reward.* We have already noted that our wife is a gift from God. He says to us, "This is my daughter. Lead her, love her, care for her, and walk with her to the gates of heaven. Do this for me!"

Our children are also a gift from God. He says, "This is my precious gift! Teach them, train them, love them, protect them, care for them on my behalf. Do this for me! Teach them about my love, about my grace, about my provision, about my world, about the hope that comes through faith, about the cross where sin is atoned, about a life of faithfulness. Teach them how to love me, how to love others, how to tell the truth, how to work hard and how to glorify my Name!"

So, how do we do that?

Deuteronomy 6:1-9

Way back in Deuteronomy 6, God gave specific instructions on the raising of godly children.

1 "Now this is the commandment—the statutes and the rules—that the LORD your God commanded me to teach you, that you may do them in the land to which you are going over, to possess it, 2 that you may fear the LORD your God, you and your son and your son's son, by keeping all his statutes and his commandments, which I command you, all the days of your life, and that your days may be long. 3 Hear therefore, O Israel, and be careful to do them, that it may go well with you, and that you may multiply greatly, as the LORD, the God of your fathers, has promised you, in a land flowing with milk and honey.

4 "Hear, O Israel: The LORD our God, the LORD is one. 5 You shall love the LORD your God with all your heart and with all your soul and with all your might. 6 And these words that I command you today shall be on your heart. 7 You shall teach them diligently to your children, and shall talk of them when you sit in your house, and when you walk by the way, and when you lie down, and when you rise. 8 You shall bind them as a sign on your hand, and they shall be as frontlets between your eyes. 9 You shall write them on the doorposts of your house and on your gates.

In the first 3 verses God gave the people of Israel the reasons they were to obey the commands of God. Did you notice them? Here they are:

- That they may fear the Lord their God
- That their days may be long in the land
- That it may go well with them
- That they may greatly multiply and enjoy God's promises

While those reasons may seem to be very specific to the people of Israel, notice the phrase in verse 2 – *that you may fear the Lord your God, you and your son and your son's son.* Let's make this personal: *That you* (your name) *may fear the Lord your God, you and your son* (son's name) *and your son's son* (grandson's name).

So, what is the command? *Hear, O Israel: The Lord our God is one. You shall love the Lord your God with all your heart and with all your soul and with all your might* (6:4-5). This is the same command that Jesus gave in response to the lawyer who asked, *"What is the greatest commandment in the Law?"* (Matthew 22:36). Jesus said, *You shall love the Lord your God with all your heart and with all your soul and with all your mind. This is the great and first commandment* (22:37-38).

This is the very heart of what we need to teach our children. They need to know what it means to love the Lord with all their heart, soul, and mind.

How are they to learn this? How are we supposed to teach them this? Deuteronomy 6:6-9 tells us of six ways to do this. First, we teach through our own commitment to love the Lord God above all else. *And these words that I command you shall be on YOUR heart* (6:6).

We cannot expect to teach our children to love the Lord unless it is written on our heart and commands our thoughts, desires, decisions, actions, and relationships. To love God is to treasure and value and desire Him above all else. It does not mean meeting His needs, for hehas none. It does not mean doing things for Him.

To love God is to value and treasure Him above all else – even above our ministry. To love Him is to make Him the treasure of your life and your greatest desire and joy.

How do we do that? Reflect on His grace! Enjoy His grace! Rest in His grace!

Next, we teach our children through purposeful teaching times. *You shall teach them DILIGENTLY to your children* (6:7).

This is not the teaching of someone else (Sunday school teachers) but speaks of a careful, planned and consistent teaching time that you leader as a father. God has given the responsibility for child training to parents and primarily fathers. It is not someone else's job – it is yours!

Then, we teach our children through our daily conversation. You *shall TALK of them when you sit in your house, and when you walk by the way, and when you lie down, and when you rise* (6:7). Everything we say must reflect the love we have for the Lord. All the daily conversation we have as a family ought to reflect your love for the Lord. Not just on Sunday on the way to church. Not just at planned teaching times. But every conversation must point our children to the love we have for the Lord.

Next, we teach our children through our daily activities. *You shall bind them as a sign on your HAND* (6:8). This includes the way we do our business. This means our love for the Lord is seen in how we treat people in the market, how we handle our money and what we watch on television. Everything we do must reflect our love for the Lord.

Next, we teach our children through our view of the world. The words of God *shall be frontlets between your EYES*. The world is filled with problems. There are political problems, financial problems, business problems. But do we view our world in light of our love for the Lord or in light of our love for ourselves. What do our children learn about love for the Lord when they hear us speak of how we see the world around us? Do they hear us speak of the sovereignty of the Lord? Do they hear us speak of our trust in him as the Lord God? Do they hear what it means to submit to those in authority over us?

Finally, we teach our children through our dealings with the community. *You shall write them on the doorposts of your house and on your gates* (6:9). What do our children learn about our love for the Lord as they watch us relate to our relatives, to our neighbors or to those who do not like us or even persecute us? Do our children hear and see that we love the Lord? What do our children learn when someone steals something valuable of ours, or breaks into our home? Do they learn that the Lord is our greatest treasure, or that our things are more precious to us than he is?

We live in a world that is filled with gods. The gods may not be those made of wood or stone. They may not be in the shape of pagan shrines and altars. But even as believers we have a surprising number of idol altars in our homes and in our pursuits, and too often, we teach our children to bow at those altars. There is the altar of academic success. The altar of sports and recreation. The altar of clothing or fashion. The altar of bigger and better things. The altar of latest music and TV stars. The altar of financial success and the altar of superstition.

But how often do we teach them to bow at the altar of the King of kings and Lord of lords? Do we spend as much time intentionally leading our children to follow God as we do to be successful in other pursuits?

We must refuse to allow trivial, temporal pursuits to interfere with the main thing. No academic achievement, sports endeavor, clothing and fashion, music, TV program or financial gain will ever be as important as helping our children to become men or women of God.

Our children do not belong to us, they belong to God. And God has asked us to bring them up to be followers of Him and His Word. God has asked us to be the ones that teach them what it means to love the Lord God with all their heart, soul and mind.

The Role of a Father

A study of the New Testament will reveal three passages that teach about the role of the father.

> *Fathers, do not provoke your children to anger, but bring them up in the discipline and instruction of the Lord* (Ephesians 6:4).

> *Fathers, do not provoke your children, lest they become discouraged* (Colossians 3:21).

> *For you know how, like a father with his children, we exhorted each one of you and encouraged you and charged you to walk in a manner worthy of God* (1 Thessalonians 2:11-12).

It is important to notice that fathers are entrusted with the overall responsibility of both the training and discipline of the children. Their mother may play a major role in the process, but this is a job given to fathers. This is a significant part of managing your household well.

How are we supposed to do this job? In 1 Thessalonians 2:11-12 we have the example of Paul that gives the following:

- **We are to Exhort.** This is to call on or to urge them to take a course of action.
- **We are to Encourage.** We are to take time to come alongside, to walk with them through the experiences of life, like the Holy Spirit who walks with us through life.
- **We are to Charge.** We are to give clear and careful instruction using our words and our example.

This is not a responsibility that is to be taken lightly. This training must be serious and intentional. It does not and will not happen by itself. We must be careful to build it into our schedules. It will not happen by itself.

Bruce Ware points out that fathers have two sinful tendencies.[23] The first is to abuse our power by being heavy handed, nasty, harsh, and demanding in unloving and selfish ways. He writes,

> God has not given men this authority in our homes for the purpose of gratifying our own pleasures and exploiting the opportunity for our ease and comfort. Rather, such authority must be exercised out of benevolence. A position of headship must be used to promote healing, life, restoration, growth, prospering and joy.

Have you ever noticed what children do when we abuse our position of authority? Ephesians 6:4 says they become angry.

---

[23] Ware, *Father, Son, and Holy Spirit*, 142.

Colossians 3:21 says they become discouraged. These are not just Bible verses but the experience of too many children who are not cared for by their fathers.

The second sinful tendency of fathers is the abdication of their responsibility to be involved in the training of their children. They are not actively involved with them, or they leave all the training to others in the community, school, church or family. But this is the task of fathers and it seems we must be reminded again and again because we find it so easy to leave this to other people. To manage our household well, so that our children are submissive and become believers in the Lord Jesus Christ means that we must be active, involved and giving loving and gentle leadership to the process. This takes time!

This also takes modeling by a father. According to data collected by Baptist Press, if a mother doesn't go to church but the father does, approximately two-thirds of their children will continue to attend church in adulthood. By contrast, if the mother attends church but the father doesn't, two-thirds of the children will drop out of church completely, and only 1 in 50 will become a regular worshipper.[24] If we want our children to continue in their relationship with the Lord and participate in the life and ministry of the church, they need to see it regularly and consistently in us.

The Role of a Mother

Mothers also have a role in training children. Mothers are to partner with her husband in the training process, since children are to be taught to obey both parents. Mother are to be the father's helper in training our children, making up what he lacks.

---

[24] Nick Cady, "The Impact on Kids of Dad's Faith and Church Attendance," Theology for the People, https://nickcady.org/2016/06/20/the-impact-on-kids-of-dads-faith-and-church-attendance/, June 20, 2016. Accessed May 30, 2022.

To accomplish this task, you and your wife need to establish a training partnership. You need to agree together on what you will teach and how you will teach it. You need to agree together on what you will use as appropriate discipline. You need to agree together that you will not undermine each other in front of the children.

Mothers need to remember that it is their husband who is responsible to God for the leadership and direction of his family. Even when Eve sinned in the Garden of Eden, God charged Adam with failure to lead his family. In Genesis 3:17 God told Adam, "Because you did not take leadership of your family, cursed is the ground because of you." Wives and mothers are not responsible before God for the direction of their family, but they are charged with helping their husband fulfill the responsibility God has given him. Mothers bring a softer element to the task in that she is portrayed as the one who nurtures and tenderly loves. In 1 Thessalonians 2:7 Paul describes a mother this way: *But we were gentle among you, like a nursing mother taking care of her own children.*

Training Children

What do children need to learn? There are lot of things. They need to learn to walk, feed themselves, to talk, to dress themselves, and to clean up after themselves. They need to learn to listen, to read, to write, to be appropriately creative and to work. They need to learn to use their personalities and invest their physical energy in healthy activities.

The most important thing they must learn is that they need to embrace the faith and learn to love the Lord God with all their hearts, souls, and minds. How do they learn that? Read the Bible to them. It is God's voice into their lives. It is God's primary tool in preparing them for a life of godliness and service (2 Timothy

3:17). The Bible is the agent or the means by which God will conform them to the image of Christ (2 Peter 2:4).

Encourage them to ask questions. Read good books to them; books that will teach them and help them understand God and his work in the world. Give them books that will help them think biblically and books that will connect them to the church and its history. Insist on and model church attendance as a priority over all other events and opportunities.

Our task as fathers is not complete until the faith is embraced and a transition into the church family has been made. Our goal is not just to raise healthy, mature young adults, but to raise the next generation of faithful men and women committed to being and building the church of Christ.

Our children also need relationship training. One of the best ways for children to learn how to build relationships and respect for others will be taught and caught through the child's observation of how you treat their mother. In addition, children will copy your example as you interact with friends, neighbors, the authorities. What they see you do; they will often repeat.

In a culture where role distinctions are being lost, we must also teach our children what it means to be a man and a woman. If we expect our children to enjoy marriages and families under the blessing of God we must not allow our culture to redefine the nature of manhood and womanhood. We will need to be aware of what they are being taught in school and on the playground and counter it with God's beautiful design and promises for families.

The purpose of biblical parenting is to teach wisdom which begins with "fear of the Lord" (Prov. 1:7). Every child must decide between two ways: the way of wisdom or the way of folly. It is our responsibility as parents to direct our child from their early life, toward the way of wisdom through careful instruction and through its display in the life of the parents.

We cannot leave this until later in life. It must begin when they are small children, even before school starts for them. Proverbs 22:6 instructs us to *Train up a child in the way he should go; even when he is old he will not depart from it.* In his book *God, Marriage, and Family,* Andreas Köstenberger makes this comment about Proverbs 22:6,

> While this verse should not be considered a divine promise, it is the product of keen and solid observation of what usually occurs in life, and this should be taken seriously. In the end, however, children do make their own decisions as to which way they want to go. Most likely, once grown, children will tend to follow in the path they were shown when still a child. This is why parental discipline and instruction are so important, and why obedience and respect for authority must be infused in a child during his or her formative years."[25]

Köstenberger goes on to suggest the following lessons for children from Proverbs that need to be taught and modeled by parents as they seek to lead their children into the way of wisdom.[26]

Lessons	Proverbs
Diligence and hard work	6:6-11; 11:27; 12:24; 13:4; 15:19; 18:9; 19:24; 20:4, 13; 21:5; 22:13; 26:13-16
Justice	11:1; 16:11; 17:23; 20:10, 23; 31:8-9
Kindness	11:17
Generosity	11:24; 19:6
Self-Control of Speech	12:18; 13:3; 21:23
Self-Control of Temper	14:17, 29; 15:18; 16:32; 19:11; 25:28
Righteousness	12:21, 28; 14:34

---

[25] Andreas J. Köstenberger and David W. Jones, *God, Marriage & Family: Rebuilding the Biblical Foundation* (Wheaton, Ill: Crossway Books, 2004), 103.

[26] Adapted from IBID., 104.

Lessons	Proverbs
Truthfulness and honesty	12:22; 16:13; 16:30; 17:20; 24:26
Discretion in choosing friends	13:20; 18:24
Discretion in choosing a spouse	18:22; 31:10-31
Caution and prudence	14:16; 27:12
Gentleness	15:1, 4
Contentment	15:16-17; 16:8; 17:1
Integrity of character	15:27; 28:18
Humility	16:19; 18:12; 22:4
Graciousness	16:24
Restraint	17:14, 27-28; 18:6-7; 29:20
Faithfulness in all things	28:20
Faithfulness in friendships	17:17
Purity	20:9; 22:11
Vigorous pursuit of what is good and right	20:29
Skillfulness in work	22:29
Patience	25:15
To refrain from a pleasure-seeking lifestyle	21:7
To refrain from partying and gluttonous eating and drinking	23:20-21; 28:7
Not to be arrogant or vain	21:24

Disciplining Children

The training of children must include discipline. Discipline is not designed to merely punish a child for an offense but must be "future-oriented and forward looking."[27] The primary purpose is not just immediate compliance but long-term progress toward becoming a mature and responsible adult.

Discipline must be consistent. Discipline must be balanced. Children must be kept under control, being required to obey authority. On the other hand, parents need to be careful not to be harsh or make their children angry by announcing or changing the rules after the offense. This will cause them to lose heart and give

---

[27] IBID, p. 161

up on obedience.

Discipline must be fair. It must fit the offence. It must be age and child specific. Each child is different and must be treated as an individual. The same disciplinary action will not fit every child.

Discipline must not be about our anger but about loving guidance. Discipline is not for revenge or to express our anger at their childishness or disobedience. We discipline out of love for our child and fear of the consequences of disobedience.

Discipline must also be relational. It must be practiced in the context of a relationship with the child. Discipline is most effective when the child feels secure in the caring, loving, tender and friendly relationship they have with the parents.

How Not to Provoke Your Children to Anger

John Piper suggests there are at least eight things to avoid when trying to get our children to obey.[28] These are worth taking note of.

- **Nagging**. Don't try to get obedience by repetitive demands or requirement that are annoying and demeaning. Instead, give your instructions once, being careful that the child understands what you want.

- **Demanding**. Don't try to get obedience by being a father who only demands. Instead, clearly explain what you want and why you want it. Complement the child and celebrate what the child has done.

- **Getting Angry**. Don't try to get obedience by setting a tone where every requirement sounds angry. Be cheerful as you ask your children to do something.

- **Always Resorting to the Rod**. Don't try to get obedience

---

[28] "How Do I Not Provoke My Children?," *Desiring God*, n.d., accessed May 25, 2022, https://www.desiringgod.org/interviews/how-do-i-not-provoke-my-children.

by always resorting to physical threats. Don't make slapping or hitting part of your motivation for obedience.

- **Embarrassing**. Don't try to get obedience by embarrassing the child in front of other people. Find ways to make your requests respectful and polite.

- **Belittling**. Don't try to get obedience by belittling your child. Don't call them names or speak in a way that makes them feel like you do not like them.

- **Requiring the Impossible**. Don't demand things that are impossible for the child to do at their age. Don't set them up for automatic failure. If it is a new task or responsibility, take the time to patiently show and teach them what you want.

- **Withholding Forgiveness**. Don't try to get obedience without creating an atmosphere of forgiveness. Teach them that when they fail there is a way for them to be forgiven, just as Christ has forgiven you. You must speak the gospel and teach the gospel, so that the child understands how the blood of Jesus gives forgiveness and life and relief. You must embody the gospel in your own confession of sin and failure, even to the child you have failed. You must continually offer your own forgiveness to them.

Children With Special Needs

Children are a gift from the Lord (Psalm 127:3). Each one is a special treasure God has entrusted to our care and discipleship. Some of those children are extra-special treasures that need extra-special time-consuming care. These are the children with special needs.

Lauren Garcia writes,

Special needs can mean many things — from thriving with a condition that challenges a single aspect of daily life to coping with something that forces you to learn a new normal. The term "special needs" is used to describe a person with a physical or emotional difficulty or difference that requires more assistance or specialized services.[29]

She goes on to define the four main categories of special needs:

- **Physical:** Multiple sclerosis, allergies and asthma, juvenile arthritis, leukemia, muscular dystrophy, epilepsy.

- **Developmental:** Down syndrome, autism, dyslexia, dyscalculia, dysgraphia, dyspraxia, aphasia or dysphasia, auditory processing disorder, visual processing disorder.

- **Behavioral/emotional:** Obsessive compulsive disorder, dissociation, post-traumatic stress disorder, anxiety, depression, attention deficit (hyperactivity) disorder, bipolar.

- **Sensory-impaired:** Blindness, deaf or limited hearing, visually impaired.

Each of these children bring challenges and caring for them takes additional time and energy. Some of the most common characteristics of parents with special needs children are the feelings of being alone, tiredness, and hopelessness. Theirs is often a difficult journey that is complicated and confusing.

As an elder or an aspiring elder who is employed outside of the church, if your family has been blessed with the opportunity to love and care for a special needs child, it will be essential for

---

[29] Lauren Garcia, "Special Needs: Defining and Understanding the 4 Types," *Care.Com Resources*, March 18, 2022, accessed June 29, 2022, https://www.care.com/c/types-of-special-needs/.

you to understand the amount of time you will need to invest at home. This may have implications on how much time you can dedicate to eldering. Since our responsibility is to manage our own household well, you may need to limit the amount of time you invest in giving leadership to the rest of the church family.

But having a special needs child in your home can also be a blessing to others in the church family who also have special needs children. Since you understand their difficulties, you can be an encouragement as well as an advocate for them. While your ministry impact may be limited by time, it will be magnified as you walk with others who share the same load. Your advocacy for them with the other elders and ministry leaders will go a long way in helping the church family understand and better meet the needs of these families.

Sarah Walton gives this encouragement,

> As much as we would like answers and help for the often overwhelming circumstances surrounding our children, we must remember that God himself is the answer that we need in both an earthly and spiritual sense. He knows each member of our family intimately and is working out his good purposes in each of our lives (including our precious children with special needs), often in ways we would never have expected. As we learn to trust Christ and find joy amidst what seems senseless and hopeless to the world around us, we will draw others to the hope of the gospel.
>
> If you have been given the privilege and responsibility of raising a child that has taken you to the end of yourself, I pray that you will be strengthened by remembering that your precious family has been divinely chosen to display God's glorious redemptive story. Although we aren't promised healing on this earth, we are promised that

Christ will not waste one tear we shed over these painful effects of sin within our world.

You are not hopeless, you are not alone, and you are not defined by your child's disorder. Rather, you have been called and entrusted to raise a child with special needs for the glory of God. Through the grace of Jesus Christ, he can take and use what seems devastating to drive you to him, mold you to his image, bring unexpected blessing, and display his glory through your life and story.[30]

---

[30] Sarah Walton, "To Parents with Special Needs," *Desiring God*, July 14, 2017, accessed June 29, 2022, https://www.desiringgod.org/articles/to-parents-with-special-needs.

Application Questions or Activities

1. How would you measure your leadership at home? Use the chart below for your evaluation.

<table>
<tr><td colspan="5">Godly Leadership at Home</td></tr>
</table>

One who demonstrates godly leadership in his own home.

> *... he must manage his own family well*
>
> *... and see that his children obey him with proper respect* (1 Tim. 3:4)
>
> *... a man whose children believe*
>
> *... and are not open to the charge of being wild and disobedient* (Titus 1:6)

An elder must preside over a well-ordered home. The most reliable means of determining the quality of one's spiritual leadership is to examine the life and behavior of his children. They are not expected to be perfect, but to give evidence that he knows how to instruct and discipline them. If a man cannot minister to his own children, how can be expected to be effective in leading others to faith and maturity in Christ?

Weak				Strong
1	2	3	4	5

2. As you review the qualities outlined above how do you measure up? Has weakness in any of these areas disqualified you from leadership at this time? Where do you need to keep growing? What do you need to do and are you going to do to progress toward godliness in these areas?

3. How serious are you taking your role as a father? Are you abdicating your responsibility? Or are you hands-off and delegate responsibility to their mother or others in the community? What would it look like and what changes would you need to make in your life and schedule to be more actively involved?

4. What are the most important things you need to teach your children? Why have you chosen these?

5. How are you doing in teaching your children? Do you have an intentional plan for doing this? If you do not have a plan, take some time to make a list of the things you want your children to learn and how you might teach those things.

6. If your children were to share, what would they say about your training? What would they say is the most important thing they have learned from you?

7. How are your children doing spiritually? Do you even know? Do your children know and understand God's grace? Do they live in awe of the Lord Jesus? Do they love the Word of God? What are the best ways you can teach them these things?

Chapter 4: The Rest of Your Household

In the language of the New Testament a household was much larger than a single family made up of a mother and father and children. A household included more than the family who lived in a particular house. It encompassed people who were connected to that family, including other close family members, neighbors, employees, colleagues and even servants. To manage our household well we need to also interact with all these relationships in a manner that is pleasing to God.

Your Close Family

Part of the package of being born into a family are the relatives. Later in life, when we get married, this group of people grows even larger. These people come in all sizes and shapes. They come with all kinds of ideas, values, theologies, opinions, and ways of doing things. Some we appreciate and love to spend time with. Others we are not so fond of and would like to avoid. But, like it or not, these people are part of our household. Fathers, mothers, sisters, brothers, grandparents, aunts, uncles, and cousins are all part of the package of life.

God places a high value on family. Newman writes,

> He calls himself "Father, Son, and Holy Spirit." He could have chosen terms other than ones related to family. But he didn't. Even though the title of "father" is found less often in the Old Testament than in the New, it is not out of place in the books of the law, the prophets, and the writings. The notion that God can be understood as a caring, nurturing, protecting Abba pervades both testaments. Just one example, a rather substantial one, should suffice for our argument. When the prophet Isaiah arrived at that climactic

moment of his Immanuel prophecy, declaring that the Messiah will be with us, he revealed God's trust-inspiring titles of "Wonder-Counselor, Almighty-God, Eternal-Father, Prince-of-Peace" (Isa. 9:6, my translation). Right there in the midst of some of the loftiest titles of deity stands the label "Father."[31]

Throughout the New Testament, family language is used to help us grasp the truths being taught. The church is called the "Bride of Christ." Those who come to faith in Christ are called "sons" or "children of God" who have been "adopted" (Romans 8:15-16). Men and women in the church family are referred to as "brothers" and "sisters."[32] When Christ returns, we are told we will celebrate with him at the "marriage supper" (Revelation 19:9). This means we must see our family as a God-designed institution and not merely as a group of people brought together by birth or marriage. Families are God's plan and our family is part of his plan.

We also need to clearly see who we ought to be in our family relationships. Since God is relational and is willing to sacrifice himself for others, we need to be less self-oriented and more other-oriented in our family relationships. We are not part of a family so that we can get something from them, like an inheritance, but so we can give something. What we give is ourselves. This includes sharing our time, money, energy, support, faith, wisdom, and encouragement with them.

Families also serve as God's discipleship school. Newman asks us to "Consider the many verses in Proverbs that portray the family as the setting for promoting wisdom, developing

---

[31] Newman, Randy. Bringing the Gospel Home (pp. 27-28). Crossway. Kindle Edition.

[32] In the New Testament, depending on the context, the plural Greek word *adelphoi* which is translated "brothers" may refer to brothers and sisters.

discernment, acquiring prudence, and establishing the fear of the Lord."[33] The first nine chapters of Proverbs is a letter from a father to a son, exhorting him to seek wisdom. Family is the training center God often uses to form character as members watch each other, both in close and extended family, and modeling what it means to walk in the ways of the Lord.

As you manage your household, don't do it independently of other family members. Employ their wisdom, experience, understanding, skill, and commitment to godliness to help you fulfill your responsibilities as a family leader.

How are we to manage these family relationships when they are difficult? Stacy Reaoch, who co-authored the book *Making Room for Her: Biblical Wisdom for a Healthier Relationship with Your Mother-In-Law or Daughter-In-Law,* gives this advice for navigating difficult family relationships:[34]

- **Pray for your own heart**. Ask God to soften your heart towards this person, to put off anger and irritability, to put on meekness and kindness, to understand this person's struggles and meet them with compassion (Colossians 3:12–14).

- **Pray for them**. Ask God to be at work in their hearts, drawing unbelievers to himself and sanctifying believers to become more like Jesus (Philippians 1:9–11).

- **Move toward them, not away from them**. Although our tendency is to want to steer clear of people with whom we have strained relationships, they are exactly the people we need to be intentionally moving toward. Find ways to engage them in conversation, meet them for

---

[33] Ibid, 31.

[34] Stacy Reaoch, "Loving Difficult People", https://www.desiringgod.org/articles/loving-difficult-people, May 5, 2015. Accessed June 2, 2022.

coffee, send them a text.

- **Find specific ways to bless and encourage them.** Write them a note of appreciation. Buy them a book that has been an encouragement to you. Tell them you are praying for them.

- **Give them grace, just as God extends grace to you.** Remember God's lavish grace poured out for your own daily sins. Ask God to help you bear with them, forgiving them, as he has forgiven you (Colossians 3:13).

- **Realize that you too could be the difficult person in someone else's life!** You might not even realize that you are a thorn in the flesh for someone close to you. Don't be oblivious to your own shortcomings and sins.

Before we close our discussion on family relationships, there is one caution that needs to be noted. When we make our family more important than God or his kingdom, we distort family. Newman says,

> The family cannot fulfill its God-given purpose if we demand from it things which only God can provide. Such unrealistic demands from spouses, parents, children, or any other relationship cause it to be a source of pain or bitterness or alienation instead of joy, security, and intimacy.[35]

Jesus made it very clear that our second birth takes priority over our first birth. Our ultimate allegiance is to the Lord Jesus and our trust must be in him and his promises. While very important in life, our family cannot give us what Jesus can only give. Don't worship your family and don't put pressure on it to be perfect. We need to find our ultimate completeness, joy, and peace in who we

---

[35] Ibid, 39.

have become in God's family through faith in Christ. This reference point will guide us as we manage our families well.

Your Neighbors

Since we are not physically taken out of the world when we come to faith in Christ, how are we to live in and relate to our world and the people who live around us? How do we manage our household well in terms of our neighbors?

In his prayer for his disciples in John 17, Jesus says three things about our relationship to the world (17:13-21). One, he says the world will hate his followers because they are not of the world. Just as they hated Christ, we can expect some will hate us because we are not like them. Two, we won't be taken out of the world just because we are believers, but we can expect our Father to protect us from the evil one. Three, we are sent into the world just as Christ was sent into the world.

What are we sent to do? The same thing Christ was sent to do: to witness to the truth of the gospel. We do that with our actions and words because we are to proclaim the praises of the one who called us out of darkness into his marvelous light (1 Peter 2:9).

According to Luke 10:25-37, one day a lawyer, trying to trap Jesus, asked him this question: "Teacher, what shall I do to inherit eternal life?" Jesus answered him with this question: "What is written in the Law? How do you read it?" The lawyer knew the Law well and responded, "You shall love the Lord your God with all your heart and with all your soul and with all your strength and with all your mind, and your neighbor as yourself." Jesus responded, "You have answered correctly; do this and you will live." As lawyers are known to do, he tried to evade the implication of God's demand and came back with a question: "And who is my neighbor?"

Jesus used the opportunity to tell the parable of a man who was traveling from Jerusalem to Jericho. Along the way he ran into bandits who stole what he had, beat him up, and left him half-dead at the side of the road. Sometime later a priest came across the man, but instead of helping him, he simple walked by on the other side of the road. Later a Levite also saw the beaten man and crossed the road as he passed by. But a Samaritan, someone despised by the Jewish community, saw the man, had compassion on him and took care of him at great expense of time and money. At the end of the parable Jesus asked, "Which of these three proved to be a neighbor to the man who fell among the robbers? The lawyer correctly responded that it was the one who showed him mercy. Jesus' parting words were, "You go, and do the same for others."

As we go about our business, as we raise our families, as we build relationships with the people around us, as we interact with our neighbors, we are to show mercy. We are to treat them with the same kind of love and mercy Jesus has shown us.

We are also to *Go, therefore, and make disciples of all nations, baptizing them in the name of the Father and of the Son and of the Holy Spirit, teaching them to observe everything I have commanded you. And remember, I am with you always, to the end of the age* (Matthew 28:19-20).

We are called to spread our influence well beyond our own community knowing that we have been given authority to speak on behalf of Jesus and that he accompanies us in our going. We have been given the responsibility of being ambassadors who speak on behalf of Christ (2 Corinthians 5:20). When we share the gospel, God is making his appeal through us. As believers, we are to actively partner with each other in the task of making disciples of all nations. We do that by going to our neighbors and by sending out missionaries who go to other nations.

As we live in our community, we are charged to abstain from sinful desires that wage war against the soul. Conduct yourselves honorably among the Gentiles, so that when they slander you as evildoers, they will observe your good works and will glorify God on the day he visits (1 Peter 2:11-12). We are to live the remaining time on earth no longer for human desires, but to do God's will. For there has already been enough time spent in doing what the Gentiles chose to do: carrying on in unrestrained behavior, evil desires, drunkenness, orgies, carousing, and lawless idolatry (1 Peter 4:2-3).

Your Work[36]

Managing your household also includes managing your work. In Ephesians 6, Paul says,

> *Bondservants, obey your earthly masters with fear and trembling, with a sincere heart, as you would Christ, not by the way of eye-service, as people-pleasers, but as bondservants of Christ, doing the will of God from the heart, rendering service with a good will as to the Lord and not to man, knowing that whatever good anyone does, this he will receive back from the Lord, whether he is a bondservant or is free* (Ephesians 6:5-8).

Since we do not endorse slavery, how does this relate to a conversation about a believer in the workplace? To help us understand slavery in the first century Roman world, Harold Hoehner writes,

> In the first century slaves worked in many sectors of the economy. They were used in various types of agriculture and industry, as potters and miners of gold and silver. Other occupations were public cooks, fullers (laundry), couch

---

[36] Adapted from Daryl Kroeker, *Gripping the Essentials*, 127-129.

makers, and bakers; in the professions they were business agents and teachers, and in large households, accountants, and physicians. Also, the Roman state owned slaves to carry out municipal services. Emperors used them throughout the empire in various capacities and some even managed and maintained the imperial properties. In the imperial palace slaves were used as physicians, chamberlains, overseers of furniture and palace lighting, selectors of jewelry for specific costumes, valets, tailors and clothing menders, butlers in charge of wine for the imperial table, official tasters, and stewards in charge of supplies. The use of slaves was pervasive in the first century of the Roman Empire. Ephesian slaves would have served in many of these capacities.[37]

Kent Hughes adds,

Slaves under Roman law in the first century could generally count on eventually being set free. Very few ever reached old age as slaves. Slave owners were releasing slaves as such a rate that Augustus Caesar introduced legal restrictions to curb the trend. Despite this, inscriptions indicate that almost 50 percent of slaves were freed before the age of thirty. What is more, while the slave remained his master's possession he could own property – including other slaves! – and completely controlled his own property, so that he could invest and save to purchase his own freedom.[38]

It is into this context Paul writes. He does not defend slavery, nor does he attack it or demand its abolition. This is not the point of the passage. Instead, the passage is seeking to address what it

---

[37] Harold W. Hoehner, *Ephesians: An Exegetical Commentary* (Grand Rapids, Mich: Baker Academic, 2002), 803.

[38] R. Kent Hughes, *Ephesians: The Mystery of the Body of Christ* / R. Kent Hughes. (Wheaton, Illinois: Crossway Books, 2013), 204.

means to walk wisely in this relationship in which many of the believers would have found themselves.

Paul gives us five phrases to describe a believer's role in the workplace. Though they are couched in the picture of first century slavery, they are very applicable to today's workplace. First, they are to obey, or do what they are told with *fear and trembling* (6:5). In the New Testament, Paul is the only writer to use this expression (1 Cor. 2:3; 2 Cor. 7:15; Phil. 2:12), and each time he does the phrase has to do with an attitude of reverence and awe or godly fear of standing in the presence of God on the final day.[39] Paul does not mean they were to serve in fear of their masters, but they should serve in reverence as if they were in the presence of Christ. Their demeanor should be defined by the phrase *as you would Christ* found at the end of verse 5. Paul is saying, "Recognize your position in society, but also remember who your ultimate master is."

Second, they were to serve with a sincere heart (6:5). They were to have a sincere attitude. They were to put their hearts into the work they were asked to do.

Third, they were to serve to please Christ (6:5). He was to be seen as the ultimate master for whom they worked. Every task ought to be done without distinction between the secular and sacred but done under Christ's lordship in order to please him.

Fourth, slaves were to obey not merely when they were being watched, or only to please people (6:6). They were to serve from the inner being as people who were slaves of Christ and committed to the will of God. Fifth, they were to serve with a good attitude so that the Lord would benefit from their service (6:7). How might the Lord benefit? He would be well-spoken of.

---

[39] Peter Thomas O'Brien, *The Letter to the Ephesians,* The Pillar New Testament Commentary (Grand Rapids, Mich.: Eerdmans, 2009), 449–450.

The glory of his character would be displayed through the worker.

Why should a slave obey his earthly master? Why should an employee work hard for his employer? Because they know their Master in heaven is going to reward them (6:8). Faithful service is not just to receive the benefit of our work on earth in the form of praise or payment, but to receive a reward from the Lord. Paul tells us that whatever we do, we are to do it all for the glory of God (1 Corinthians 10:31).

In summary, how is an employee to serve their employer? We are called to be respectful (*obey*), sincere (*with a sincere heart*), conscientious *(not by way of eye-service, as people pleasers)*, pleasant (*with good will*), focused on the Lord (*as to the Lord and not man*) and expectant of God's blessing *(he will receive back from the Lord)*.

If you serve as an employer or a workplace leader, Ephesians 6 also gives you instructions. Paul writes, *Masters, do the same to them, and stop your threatening, knowing that he who is both their Master and yours is in heaven, and that there is no partiality with him* (Ephesians 6:9).

When Paul tells us *to do the same to* them, he is not telling us to obey our employees, but to see them as people of equal standing. We are to treat them with respect in the same way they are to treat us with respect. Jesus went further and taught that those in authority need to adopt the role of servants toward those they lead. Jesus told his disciples,

> *"You know that those who are considered rulers of the Gentiles lord it over them, and their great ones exercise authority over them. But it shall not be so among you. But whoever would be great among you must be your servant, and whoever would be first among you must be slave of all. For even the Son of Man came not to be served but to serve, and to give his life as a ransom for many"* (Mark 10:42-45).

Can you imagine the wonderful picture of the Lord we portray when we go out of our way to serve those who work for us? I

(Daryl) had a godly employer who modeled this well. Each day that he came to the construction worksite he would meet with each of his employees individually. In that conversation he always asked about our family members by name. He inquired about our interests and our out-of-work activities and offered help with whatever problems we were struggling with. Only after these individual conversations would he go to our foreman to deal with the issues of the project we were working on. We knew we were loved and cared for by our boss, and if he needed extra time or effort from us to meet a work deadline, the answer was an easy "Yes!"

Paul also tells work leaders to *stop threatening*. For believers, there is no place to use threats as motivation. Intimidating with foul language, manipulation, threatening to fire, or threats of violence, are not to be among the leadership tools of those who manage their workplace relationships well. We are not to abuse the power of our position.

The motivation for leading well comes from the fact that God is our judge. He is the one who is the ultimate master of our employees and of us, and he will not show us partiality on the day of judgment because of our leadership position at work.

Christian employers and workplace leaders are to be respectful (*do the same to them*), sincere and encouraging (*stop your threatening*), focused on the Lord (*he who is both their Master and yours is in heaven*), and expectant of the Lord's blessing (*there is no partiality with him*).

As we summarize this chapter there are two traits Paul gives in 1 Timothy 3 that are important to remember. One is that the man who aspires to church leadership must *be above reproach* (3:2). The other Paul gives us is that *he must be well thought of by outsiders, so that he may not fall into disgrace, into the snare of the devil* (3:7).

The term *above reproach* is similar to being *blameless* as required in Titus 1:6. This is not a demand for sinless perfection, but it means we should be the kind of man who has no obvious or provable black stains against our character.[40] Since we have been declared blameless or righteous through God's work of grace in justification (Colossians 1:22), we are to live consistent with what grace has conferred on us.

Those outside the church family ought to think well of us. They must see us as gracious, kind, forgiving, honest about our weaknesses, willing to face up to and correct our failures, and willing to go out of our way to show the love of Christ to those we like and do not particularly like. This is part of what it means to manage our household well.

---

[40] Yarbrough, Robert W., *The Letters to Timothy and Titus*, The Pillar New Testament Commentary, (Grand Rapids: Eerdmans), 195.

<u>Application Questions or Activities</u>

1. Make a list of those you would consider part of your close family. What kind of relationship do you have with each one? Which relationships are going well and which ones or more demanding? What can you do to make a difference in the more demanding relationships?

2. Who are your neighbors? What are you doing to actively build relationships with them? Are you regularly praying for these people? What steps can you take to communicate the gospel through your words and actions?

3. Who are the people you work with? As a believer, what is your role or responsibility in your workplace relationships? What are you doing to actively represent the gospel to those who are not believers?

4. How do you think the people in these relationships (close family, neighbors, and workplace) would describe your character? Would they see you as being a person above reproach? Are there any outstanding sins or brokenness that you need to deal with? If there is, what is your plan to take care of these issues?

Chapter 5: Guarding Your Household

There are no perfect families. No one has ever done everything right. A pastor once said that part of parenting is failing in front of your kids so you can teach them repentance.

As believers we are all on a journey, learning to apply God's Word to our lives and our families. As we do that, we need to recognize that it is only by His grace that we succeed in our responsibilities.

Romans 3:23-25 tells us that *all have sinned and fall short of the glory of God, and are justified by his grace as a gift, through the redemption that is in Christ Jesus, whom God put forward as a propitiation by his blood, to be received by faith.* Grace is the very heart of the Bible, the heart of the Gospel and the heart of our lives!

Every day I earn more and more of God's wrath because of my sin. The longer I am a believer the more I see how truly sinful I am. The longer I live the more I appreciate the grace of the Lord Jesus. I am overwhelmed that he would die for my sins; that he would take my punishment; that he would forgive me; that he would clothe me with his righteousness; that he would adopt me as His child; and that he would take care of me day by day when all I have ever done is earn His wrath through my sin! Romans 8:1 is an amazing truth: *Now therefore this is no condemnation for those who are in Christ Jesus!*

Never grow tired of His grace! Never stop being amazed! Never stop treasuring Jesus above all else! Never stop sharing His grace with others!

We are not to take credit for success. We are only to point to the Lord Jesus Christ and thank him for his grace poured out on the cross for our redemption. Not only that, but his grace is also poured out into our lives every day as he provides strength, wisdom, understanding and patience to faithfully complete the tasks he has assigned to us as ministry leaders.

Even as we rejoice in his grace, we must not take grace for granted. There is still a place where we must be diligent. Paul told Timothy to *train yourself for godliness* (1 Timothy 4:7). He was not asking Timothy to work towards his salvation but to work at being godly. It does not come naturally.

We are in a battle. There are all kinds of forces at work that would seek to destroy our faith and the credibility of our message. There is our own selfish sin nature which still lurks within our lives. There is the pull of the world and all its enticements that call for our affections and allegiance. There is Satan and his forces which desire to bring doubt, dishonor and destruction into our lives. There is the pressure to give up on continual growth toward holiness. There is suffering that makes me want to turn away from the ministry to which I have been called.

We are in a battle, and we need to know that one of the most important places this battle is fought is in the management of our households. If Satan can destroy your marriage and your family, he will. He will do it because through your failure he can lie and declare to the world that just as your marriage failed, so too will the Lord Jesus Christ.

What can we do? How do we train ourselves to be godly? How do we discipline ourselves so that we are strong enough to stand up to our enemies?

Malachi 2:13-16 gives us an answer in terms of our families.

> *And this second thing you do. You cover the Lord's altar with tears, with weeping and groaning because he no longer regards the offering or accepts it with favor from your hand. But you say, "Why does he not?" Because the LORD was witness between you and the wife of your youth, to whom you have been faithless, though she is your companion*

and your wife by covenant. Did he not make them one, with a portion of the Spirit in their union? And what was the one God seeking? Godly offspring. So guard yourselves in your spirit, and let none of you be faithless to the wife of your youth. "For the man who hates and divorces, says the LORD, the God of Israel, covers his garment with violence, says the LORD of hosts. So guard yourselves in your spirit, and do not be faithless."

The context of this passage finds the people of Israel back in the land after their captivity in Babylon. A hundred years has gone by since the first return in 538 BC. The temple has been rebuilt but the promises of expansion, prosperity and peace that were given by Haggai and Zechariah eighty years earlier seem empty.

Instead, the people are facing economic problems, drought, crop failure and pestilence. Into this setting Malachi was called to preach a message of renewal. One of the messages he preaches concerns the breaking of the marriage covenant. In his message to husbands he challenges us to *guard yourselves in your spirit, and let none of you be faithless to the wife of your youth* (2:15).

How do we guard ourselves? The word *guard* means to make a hedge around, to protect, to exercise great care. It means to build a wall. There are several ways you need to guard yourself and your household by building walls. For purposes of simplification, we are concentrating on one specific threat against our families: sexual immorality. Most of the principles, counsel and exhortations we present as advice for protecting your marriage from sexual immorality will also protect you from all other threats to your family. Are you tempted to place your ministry before your family? These walls can protect your family from that. Are you tempted to escape into TV, video games, a hobby, or sports so much that you neglect your family? These walls will protect your family from that.

Wall One: Guard Your Mind

Let's begin by defining some terms. The first one is sexual purity. For the married it is the life-long monogamous relationship between a husband and wife. For the single it is the abstinence of all sexual relationships outside of marriage.

The second term to define is sexual immorality. This is any sexual relationship outside the bonds of a life-long monogamous relationship between a man and a woman. Sexual immorality includes sexual harassment and any sexual advance, requests, contact or verbal exchange which is of a sexual nature that is outside the boundaries of heterosexual marriage.

While it doesn't expressly fall in the category of sexual immorality, there is a the very real, but often very subtle problem commonly referred to as an emotional affair. We have already established the divine purpose of marriage and why Scripture clearly defines it as an inviolable covenant between a man and a woman. Sadly, we can violate that covenant in a myriad of ways other than just physical adultery. Physical adultery is by far the easiest to define, and few who have any respect for the tenants and promises of Scripture would deny that physical adultery is a gross violation of the marriage covenant. But anytime we develop an emotional dependency on another of the opposite sex that should be reserved only for God and our spouse, it is also a violation of the marriage covenant.

Emotional intimacy involves sharing too much – too many of your dreams and aspirations; too much of your excitement and joy; too many of your disappointments and regrets; things that are too personal for someone other than your spouse or God. It includes walking more alongside another person during your, or their suffering than with your spouse. In other words, you are depending on someone to take care of your God-sized problem of loneliness other than the spouse that God has gifted you with. Later, as we offer some counsel and suggestions as to how to guard against this specifically in your ministry relationships, consider how the suggestions would also apply to extramarital relationships in general. They will serve as safeguards against emotional adultery.

How do we build this wall to protect us from sexual and emotional failure? How do we guard our mind? First, take time to cultivate your inner life. Often those who sin have neglected in previous weeks or months or years the regular practices of Bible reading, worship, and prayer. In doing so, they have foregone the healthy self-examination these spiritual disciplines foster. In our busyness we can neglect the care and feeding of our own souls. The battle for sexual purity is won or lost not just in the noisy trenches of the world's temptations, but at home, in quietness, on our knees.

An over-full schedule and constant activity erode the soul and relationships. Busyness wears down our ability to hear, to listen to the promptings and warning signals of God's Spirit, his Word, and his people. Fatigue becomes disorienting and it makes us oblivious to what's really happening in us. It saps us of the emotional and physical energy needed to love God and others. Your relationship with God will first suffer, but it doesn't take long for your family to feel it, then your friends and shortly thereafter, your ministry. Before very long, your entire sphere of influence will suffer from your emotional and physical fatigue.

Second, limit what you read, listen to and watch. Matthew 15:19-20 says, *For out of the heart come evil thoughts, murder, adultery, sexual immorality, theft, false witness, slander. These are what defile a person.* Sexual sin never comes out of the clear blue sky. It is often the result of a long process in which a mind susceptible to sin is granted unguarded exposure to immoral input.

Our thoughts are the fabric with which we shape our character and destiny. We must actively fight off thoughts of impurity. But the key to doing this is not simply saying "I will not lust, I will not lust"—that often has the same effect as saying, "I will not think of purple elephants." We must cultivate our hearts and minds with what is godly and pure. These better thoughts will displace the others (Philippians. 4:8).

This, at least in part, is what Jesus was talking about in Luke 11:24-26: "*When the unclean spirit has gone out of a person, it passes through waterless places seeking rest, and finding none it says, 'I will return to my house from which it came.' And when it comes, it finds the house swept and put in order. Then it goes and brings seven other spirits more evil than itself, and they enter and dwell there. And the last state of that person is worse than the first.*" Even if it is possible to expel all evil thought, it is not enough. We must replace it with, *...whatever is true, whatever is honorable, whatever is lovely, whatever is commendable, if there is anything worthy of praise, think on these things* (Philippians 4:8). In other words, the only thing that can protect us from a mind consumed by unrighteousness is replacing our minds with the mind of Christ. Notice that the person from whom the demon is expelled, winds up worse off than he was. We've seen this practically lived out in at least two different ways. First, it points to the slippery slope of sin. It is a slope that begins with a small compromise allowing a thought that's "not that bad," to fester into something that we once thought we'd never think of doing. Secondly, we've seen this played out in addiction recovery repeatedly. The addict finally admits, on some level, that they have a problem, so they decide to stop. What follows, all too often, is that a pattern develops where the addict goes through a period of abstinence, then binges.

One of the saddest examples of this I (Richard) have witnessed comes from a young man I worked with early in my counselling career. He had been addicted to heroin and gone through a year-long recovery program. I began meeting with him upon his graduation from the recovery program. On his 18th birthday, about 6 months after I began working with him, his friends convinced him that he should celebrate with "one last high". Unfortunately, the young man didn't account for his system having been free of the drug for a year and a half. He took the same amount of heroin he had once built up a tolerance for, overdosed, and died. This is an extreme example, but anytime we try to expel evil and unrighteousness without replacing it with the mind of Christ, we invite greater evil and more unrighteousness into our lives.

We can't avoid all sexual stimuli, but we can keep them from taking root in us. But we can stay away from the magazine racks, video stores, advertisements, programs, images, internet pages, people, and places that tempt us to lust. *Flee from sexual immorality* (1 Cor. 6:18). Our first duty is not to resist but to run. Scripture puts it emphatically: *"Do not set foot on the path of the wicked or walk in the way of evil men. Avoid it, do not travel on it; turn from it and go on your way"* (Proverbs 4:14-15).

Randy Alcorn writes,

> Lust is fed by whatever we've deposited in our brains that it can get its claws on. What is in our brains is what we've allowed in through our senses. The images and words in our minds must come either from specific things our eyes have seen and or ears have heard or an imaginative conglomerate of such input.
>
> What kind of person we are becoming is determined by what we are taking into our brains. When we read Scripture,

good books, participate in Christ-centered discussion, or care for the needy, we are inclining ourselves toward righteousness.

Actions, habits, character, and destiny all start with a thought and thoughts are fostered by what we choose to take into our minds. That's why your most important sex organ is your brain.

Are you feeding lust or starving it? Are you feeding your passion for Christ or starving it?

Which desires will prove stronger? The ones you feed the most.[41]

Colossians 3:1-6 says,

> *If then you have been raised with Christ, seek the things that are above, where Christ is, seated at the right hand of God. Set your minds on things that are above, not on things that are on the earth. For you have died, and your life is hidden with Christ in God. When Christ who is your life appears, then you also will appear with him in glory. Put to death therefore what is earthly in you: sexual immorality, impurity, passion, evil desire, and covetousness, which is idolatry. On account of these the wrath of God is coming.*

If you move through this list backwards, do you notice the progression of sin starting with idolatry or treasuring something as more important than God? It is frightening where this can lead us.

What are you feeding through TV, internet, movies, magazines, and music?

Wall Two: Guard Your Actions

To guard your actions with a person of the opposite gender, you need to watch for warning signals. The following provide

---

[41] Randy C. Alcorn, *The Purity Principle* (Sisters, Or: Multnomah Publishers, 2003), 42–43.

warning signals about specific relationships and the potential violation of appropriate moral boundaries:

1. The publicity test: What would others think of this relationship? What would your spouse think? What would the other pastors or elders think?
2. The mental test: What are you thinking about this person? Are your thoughts pure?
3. The instinct test: How do you feel about this relationship? Do you feel right about it? Or is it wrong?
4. The time test: Does this person want too much of your time or attention?
5. The secret test: Are there any secrets between the other person and yourself that you are withholding from your spouse?

To guard your actions, you also need to count the cost of moral failure. The following consequences are adapted from Randy Alcorn as the result of sexual impurity in the life of a pastor.[42] They will:

1. Spoil the reputation of the Lord.
2. Make you have to look into the Lord's face one day and tell him why you did it.
3. Cause untold hurt to your spouse.
4. Forfeit your spouse's respect and trust.
5. Permanently injure your credibility with your children.
6. Bring great shame to your family.
7. Inflict hurt on your church and friends, especially those you have led to the Lord.
8. Bring an irretrievable loss of years of witnessing to relatives and friends.
9. Bring pleasure to Satan, God's enemy.

---

[42] Ibid., 89.

10. Expose you and your spouse to sexually transmitted diseases.
11. Discredit your name and future ministry.
12. Invoke lifelong embarrassment upon yourself.

You need to make your own list. What are the consequences of your moral failure? From time to time, you need to review and revise your list. You also need to give a copy of your list to your wife.

Wall Three: Guard Your Ministry Relationships

We need to be careful where, when and why we meet with those of the opposite sex. There is a natural bonding process in counseling that can lead to a sense of intimacy on the part of one or both.

If you are counseling with another woman, you must ask yourself, do you look forward in a special way to your appointments with this person? Do you cancel appointments with others to meet with her? Do you prefer that your coworkers not know you are meeting her again? Or do you feel flattered when seen with her in public? Do you think about her when not with her more than is necessary to pray for her and adequately prepare for your meeting with her? Do you find yourself admiring her; either her physical appearance or her character and personality more than you do your wife? Does your gaze on her linger? Do you make inappropriate or prolonged eye contact? Any of these can be warnings of an improper relationship.

It must be recognized that ministering to the needs of people demands flexibility. Situations may arise where the elder or pastor is confronted with a circumstance that demands a response outside of what would ordinarily be practiced. Such decisions should be made carefully and with open accountability to one's spouse or other ministry leader.

With this in mind, the following provide guidelines that would be wise to follow by elders and pastors for their protection and the protection of the congregation:

1. An elder or pastor should not travel alone for any reason in a vehicle with a person of the opposite gender other than their own spouse or family members. When such travel with a person is necessary for ministry purposes it should not be repeated frequently and only be done with open accountability to another ministry leader.
2. An elder or pastor working with students should never drive a student of the opposite gender home. In the case of an emergency where there is no option, parents must be notified for consent. If the parent(s) of the students can not be reached the elder or pastor should notify their spouse or another ministry leader before departing.
3. When it is necessary to meet with a student it should be done in a public place with clear communication to the parents of the intent and purpose of the meeting.
4. An elder or pastor should not have frequent pre-arranged private lunches or meetings outside of their office with a person of the opposite gender other than their own spouse or family members. When such meetings are necessary for ministry purposes, they should only be done with open accountability to another ministry leader.
5. An elder or pastor must encourage same gender care giving and mentoring within the ministry.
6. An elder or pastor should not meet with or counsel someone of the opposite gender, other than their spouse or family members, in a closed office without an

uncovered window in the door. If possible, the door should remain ajar.

7. In a culture where homosexuality and transgenderism are all too common, an elder or pastor may want to consider never meeting alone with ANYONE unless it is in a public place or there is someone else in the church building.

8. An elder or pastor should not meet alone in the evening in their office or in a home with someone of the opposite gender other than their spouse or family members.

9. An elder or pastor should not discuss or give on-going counsel regarding sexual topics beyond an initial conversation while alone with a member of the opposite gender other than their own spouse or family members.

10. Appropriate touching is a vital part of ministry but must only be used in ways that we can assure that gestures are understood. Touch should be limited to "mirroring" what the other person deems appropriate. For example, if a person extends a hand, shake the person's hand. Do not push the hand out of the way in order to give a hug. Kissing should be completely avoided in all pastoral contact.

11. An elder or pastor should quickly distance themselves from any relationship where he or she feels threatened or tempted.

Don't be proud and say that moral failure will never happen to you. When you think that, you are already on the road to failure. Why? Because God opposes the proud.

Wall Four: Guard Your Marriage

Communication is crucial. Every act of adultery begins with a deception, and most deceptions begin with seemingly innocent secrets ("she doesn't need to know this"). If you're married, regularly evaluate your relationship with your spouse. Watch for the red flags of discontentment, poor communication, and a poor sexual relationship.

Sometimes marriage problems need assistance from the outside. Yet many Christian leaders are too proud to ask for help. They stubbornly refuse to admit their struggles and get counseling—until after they fall into immorality. If your marriage or personal life is faltering, get help now before greater damage is done. The short-term cost of swallowing our pride is far less than the long-term cost of not doing so. Avail yourself of the books, tapes, videos and seminars geared to improving your marriage. Do not be afraid to seek out help from ministry partners with more mature, more stable marriages. Do not be too ashamed to seek out competent pastoral care or counseling if necessary.

Be honest with your wife. Lust thrives on secrecy. Nothing defuses lust as effectively as exposure. Honest communication between husband and wife will make them allies, not adversaries. While there is often initial pain in discussing sexual temptation, there is also some immediate relief. This allows your wife to understand you better, pray for you more effectively and be more sensitive to your needs—all of which will draw you closer together.

Wall Five: Guard with the Help of Others

Find others you can trust to help you guard your household. We need accountability partners to help us.

It is easy to talk about accountability. But it is very hard to do.

The more gifted and active we are in ministry the prouder and more independent we become. But the more leaders become prominent, the more they need accountability—yet often the less they get it. As well, the larger our ministry, the greater the battle!

Some leaders respond to the need for accountability by saying, "Don't you trust me?" Accountability initially is not about trust, but about protection. You see, I do not trust my wicked heart. Jeremiah 17:9 says, *The heart is deceitful above all things, and desperately sick or wicked.*

We need accountability for:

1. Public Life
   a. What we preach and teach
   b. How we lead the church or ministry
   c. How we handle church or ministry money
   d. How we speak about others
2. Our Private Life
   a. How we treat our wives
   b. How we lead our family
   c. Our thoughts and inner life
   d. Our devotional and prayer life
   e. Our attitudes and relationships

To be accountable is risky. It involves entrusting your reputation to others and opening yourself up to examination and even criticism. But the risks are small compared to the rewards.

Don't try to guard your household by yourself. Enlist the help of others. You do not have to do this alone.

Wall Six: Guard Against Denial

We must keep short accounts with God. When we sin, we must confess it now. Otherwise, we'll become desensitized to it and be able to go one step further next time before our dulled conscience objects. Delayed confession is the next worst thing to no confession. *"He who conceals his sins does not prosper, but whoever confesses and renounces them finds mercy"* (Prov. 28:13).

All sins should be confessed to God because he is the One most deeply offended by our sin! Sin could also be confessed to others. James tells us to *confess your sins to each other and pray for each other* (James. 5:16). Whether or not a sin is confessed to others, and if so to whom, is dependent on who is affected by the sin, who is aware or suspicious of the sinand who is able to help avoid repeating the sin.

Any Christian's immorality, or any other unrepentant sin, has a significant effect on the whole body or organization (1 Corinthians 5:6). If others have been aware of my sin, they may have been hurt by it or even worse, desensitized to sin themselves. When a sin is public, then it is appropriate that confession should be public.

Don't live in denial. If you have sinned there may be consequences on your leadership but remember 1 John 1:8-9, *If we say we have no sin, we deceive ourselves and the truth of God is not in us. If we confess our sins, he is faithful and just to forgive us our sins and to cleanse us from all unrighteousness.*

Wall Seven: Guard Your Time

If you want to guard your household, guard your time! Do not sacrifice your marriage for ministry. Too many men in the ministry have a mistress – it is the ministry itself. As they run around doing all kinds of great things for God, they are ruining their marriage.

A pastor of some notoriety stated some years ago that he limited his work schedule, without exception, to 50 hours a week. This may be a bit limiting because there will always be legitimate reasons to extend your work week on occasion (e.g. death of a beloved member of the congregation, a child in your congregation is terminally ill or suffers a tragic accident, the community you serve suffers a catastrophic natural disaster). But we agree with the principle behind this kind of time limit. Ministry is never finished. You must establish boundaries that are rarely crossed to guard your time with family, and yourself, or your ministry will consume you and your relationships.

If you have made a covenant before God with the woman who is your wife, keep it. It takes time. It takes priority time. It means you will need to set aside time for her. Married life does take extra care and time. Be sure you take it.

As married men we have two responsibilities: How to please the Lord and how to please our wife. Paul says marriage is good, but it brings with it added responsibility. To the married he calls for *good order* and to the unmarried he calls for *undivided devotion to the Lord*. (1 Corinthians 7:35).

Do not sacrifice your children for ministry. Play with them. Walk with them. Listen to them. Read to them. Hug them. Pray with them.

In conclusion, our theology does not give us an excuse or a license to sin (Romans 6:1). What it does give us is a reason to fight and to discipline ourselves to be godly.

Piper writes,

> The distinguishing mark of saving faith is *not* perfection. The mark of faith is not that I never sin sexually. The mark of faith is that I fight. I fight anything that dims my sight of Jesus as my glorious Savior. I fight anything that diminishes the fullness of the lordship of Jesus in my life. I fight anything that threatens to replace Jesus as the supreme Treasure of my life. Anything that stands between me and receiving Jesus, faith fights — not with fists or knives or

guns or bombs, but with the truth of Christ.

So, if all you can see in the cross of Jesus is a license to go on sinning, you don't have saving faith. And you need to fall on your face and plead that God would open your eyes to see the compelling glory of Jesus Christ.[43]

Your faith is worth fighting for! Your household is worth guarding!

For Single Ministry Leaders

We are aware that the church, right or wrong, has developed a culture where singleness is looked down upon in the ministry (with possibly the exception of youth, worship, or of course, singles ministry). To be sure, there are areas of ministry where singleness is not appropriate. A pastoral counsellor, for example, who often deals with struggling marriages, would probably find it problematic to be single. We are confident that when Paul tells Timothy and Titus that the ministry leader must be the husband of one wife (1 Tim. 3:2; Titus 1:6), it is simply an admonition against polygamy (and arguably divorce). He is not saying that a leader must be married. After all, as far as we know, Paul and Timothy were both single.[44]

Do not look at your singleness as a curse or a weakness, but as a blessing and strength. Nowhere is this more clearly taught than

---

[43] John Piper, "How to Deal with the Guilt of Sexual Failure for the Glory of Christ and His Global Cause," *Desiring God*, last modified January 4, 2007, accessed May 25, 2022, https://www.desiringgod.org/messages/how-to-deal-with-the-guilt-of-sexual-failure-for-the-glory-of-christ-and-his-global-cause.

[44] Admittedly, this is controversial. There are those that believe that because Paul was a member of the Sanhedrin, he had to have been married at some point (probably prior to writing 1 Corinthians). To begin with, we're not sure that Paul was a member of the Sanhedrin, though biblical and extrabiblical evidence does seem to support such an inference. For more information see: Christopher R. Smith, "Was the Apostle Paul Married or Single?" *Good Question: Reflections on Questions about the Bible* Blogpost: last modified, 29 Oct. 2018, https://goodquestionblog.com/2018/10/29/was-the-apostle-paul-married-or-single/.

1 Corinthians 7:32-34:

> *I want you to be free from anxieties. The unmarried man is anxious about the things of the Lord, how to please the Lord. But the married man is anxious about worldly things, how to please his wife, and his interests are divided. And the unmarried or betrothed woman is anxious about the things of the Lord, how to be holy in body and spirit. But the married woman is anxious about worldly things, how to please her husband.*

If you forget for a moment that this passage was written by the same man that wrote Ephesians 5:21-33 – a beautiful exaltation of, and exhortation on, marriage – you might mistakenly believe that Paul is antimarriage. He is not. He is simply saying that our relationship with Christ and his mission are more important and more urgent. Earlier in 1 Corinthians 7, Paul speaks of his singleness as a gift (v. 7) but concedes that some have different gifts than he. The context infers that the other possible gift would be the gift of a spouse. In other words, he sees both singleness and marriage as a gift from God.

Do not waste your singleness looking for the woman of your dreams. We know that this will be hard to follow through with (we were both single once, too). We know that loneliness often becomes *the* driving force in a single's life. It becomes *the* thing that singles feel they must be saved from. In one sense, this is natural. It is the way we were designed (remember our exegesis of Genesis 2:18-23 in the introduction). In other words, when you cry out to God in your loneliness for a spouse, you are saying two things: "This is not how it's supposed to be," and, "You alone, oh God, can fix this." Both of those are incredible prayers. Do not forsake them. It is entirely appropriate to keep a watchful eye out for single persons of the opposite sex with whom you can develop healthy relationships that may or may not eventually develop into a relationship that leads to marriage. Yes, it's entirely appropriate to date if you do not date someone directly under your care in ministry.

But to spend as much or more time seeking a spouse as you would caring for one, you are negating the advantages that Paul says comes with your singleness. When your prayers become saturated with your desire for a spouse at the expense of all other matters of prayer; when you spend more time evangelizing for yourself to potential dates than for Christ; when you spend more time fantasizing and pursuing potential dates than you do the ministry that you are called to by God and your church; when your desire to find a spouse reaches this level, you are not loving those under your care but instead demanding they love you. Paul would say this is a problem. You have been given the gift of singleness (at least for a season) so that you can singularly focus on your relationship with Christ and the specific mission that hehas called you to. Do not waste that. Focus whole-heartedly on using your gifts, skills, strengths, passions and calling to glorify God, both privately and publicly. Allow God to take care of your loneliness by strengthening the bond you have with him.

Do not rush into passionate relationships. Wait. Premarital sex is not only a sin against your Heavenly Father, but also an offense against your future spouse. Think of it as adultery against your future spouse. Guarding your household begins long before you have a family. Giving in to sexual temptation prior to marriage is in essence telling God that he's not capable or willing to fix your God-sized problem of loneliness; or at least he's not fixing it fast enough.

The Greek word most often used in the New Testament to speak of adultery is "pornea" from which we get our English word, "pornography". This word is a broad term that includes far more than intercourse. The line between appropriate physical touch and "pornea" is admittedly a little hazy, but it most certainly includes things like mutual masturbation and oral sex. We are convinced that it also includes viewing, touching and fondling otherwise private areas of the body as well.

A wise old pastor once told the story of a rich father of children who were just coming of age to attend school. They lived at the top of a mountain and the only way to the top was a treacherously steep, narrow, winding road with a deadly cliff to one side. The father began interviewing potential drivers. He asked of them one question: "How close can you get your horse and buggy to the edge of that road before you fall of the cliff?"

The first driver bragged, "Oh, I'm sure I'd be fine to drive within a foot of the edge."

The second said, "Oh, I could do better than that. I could get within at least six inches before getting nervous!"

The third young man thought for a minute and stated hesitantly, "Well sir, I must admit I don't rightly know how close I could get to the cliff before falling off. I've never tried." Obviously, the father chose the third young man, because he clearly was the wisest of the three. You would do well to apply such wisdom in your dating relationships.

Too often we have heard couples that "know" they are going to get married say something like: "The wedding is just a ceremony; the license just a piece of paper. We know we are already married in the eyes of the Lord." Please see this for what it is: justification for sin. The wedding is a public, lifelong commitment letting the world know that you are giving yourselves to each other – heart and body. If nothing else, the license is an act of obedience to your God-ordained government (cf. The book of Daniel; Rom. 13:1-14; Heb. 13:17; 1 Pet. 2:13-17; etc.).

For myself (Richard), I had a fiancé prior to my wife. I was convinced, and told everyone that would listen, that "God *told* me to marry her." Never allow yourself to believe that until you both say, "I do!" Do NOT presume to know the mind of God about your future unless it actually comes to pass, or he has spoken it in Scripture. In other words, unless you can find, "Thou shalt marry __________," in Scripture (which you won't), you will not know for sure marriage is the will of God until it happens.

Thank God, I was wrong about my x-fiancé! My wife is such a better "help-meet" for me than my ex-fiancé would have been, or could have been. I am a better husband to my wife than I ever could have been to my ex-fiancé, but it took us somewhere around nine months to figure that out and for most of those nine months we "knew that we knew that we knew" that we were going to get married. My experience is not unique. Granted, this may have a lot to do with the population that God has called me primarily to work with, but in my experience more couples who are at one point convinced they will be married break up prior to the wedding than those who make it to the altar. All that to say, even if you have found your future spouse, guarding your household means: *wait.*

We are aware that this admonition comes too late for many who are reading this. You have freely given your body and heart away to someone to whom it does not belong. That's what repentance is for (see our exhortation on repentance and confession in chapter one). Repentance is the conduit through which the power of God's forgiveness and grace flows to the sinner. This is no more or no less true for sexual sin as it is for any other type of sin. Repentance is the context in which we most profoundly experience the gospel and the precious truth that *God shows his love for us in that while we were still sinners, Christ died for us*

(Romans 5:8). Repentance serves as our best teacher of the message we are called to proclaim to others.

For Those Struggling with Same Sex Attraction

You need to understand the seriousness of this sin. The Bible makes it clear that giving up natural relations for unnatural ones is exchanging the truth of God for a lie and results in worshiping and serving the creature rather than the Creator (Romans 1:24). These sins are further described as the reason God hands people over to judgment (Romans 1:26-27). Timothy Tennent writes,

> Paul sees all forms of sexual impurity as a rejection of the divine design, and in this section of his argument (1:26-27) he particularly focuses on all forms of homosexual practice as a departure from God's natural design. Richard Hays makes this point well when he says, "When human beings engage in homosexual activity, they enact an outward visible sign of an inward and spiritual activity: the rejection of the Creator's design. Thus, Paul's choice of homosexuality as an illustration of human depravity is not merely random: it serves his rhetorical purpose by providing a vivid image of humanity's primal rejection of the sovereignty of God the Creator."[45]

Tennent goes on and says,

> The New Testament is consistently negative about normalizing same-sex behavior, and nowhere in the Bible are there positive or affirming portraits. The Roman culture, which was the cultural milieu in which the early church was birthed and in which Paul's letters were written,

---

[45] Timothy C. Tennent, *For the Body: Recovering a Theology of Gender, Sexuality, and the Human Body* (Grand Rapids, Michigan, [Franklin, Tennessee]: Zondervan Reflective ; [Seedbed Publishing], 2020), 151.

was rampant with homosexual practices. Paul is making a distinct contrast between the cultural practices and the moral behavior of Christians.[46]

Same sex attraction has no place in the plan of God or in Christian living and church leadership. In the Old Testament the cities of Sodom and Gomorrah were directly destroyed by God because the anger of God was stirred against them due to their unnatural sexual desires and practices (Genesis 18-19). Because of the outstanding nature of their sin and subsequent destruction, these cities are mentioned multiple times in the New Testament including Jude 1:6-7 where Jude writes,

> *And the angels who did not stay within their own position of authority, but left their proper dwelling, he has kept in eternal chains under gloomy darkness until the judgment of the great day— just as Sodom and Gomorrah and the surrounding cities, which likewise indulged in sexual immorality and pursued unnatural desire, serve as an example by undergoing a punishment of eternal fire.*

The Bible also makes it clear that we must flee from sexual immorality (1 Corinthians 6:18), to run away from it, to go in the opposite direction. This sin demands repentance. It demands serious running. It demands that your desires and passions must be put to death. To help with that process Paul reminds us of who we are. He wrote,

> *If then you have been raised with Christ, seek the things that are above, where Christ is, seated at the right hand of God. Set your minds on things that are above, not on things that are on earth. For you have died, and your life is hidden with Christ in God. When Christ who is your life appears, then you also will appear with him in glory* (Colossians 3:1-4).

Keeping this new relationship in mind, Paul goes on and tells

---

[46] Ibid., 152.

us to, *Put to death therefore what is earthly in you: sexual immorality, impurity, passion, evil desire, and covetousness, which is idolatry. On account of these the wrath of God is coming* (Colossians 3:5-6).

1 Corinthians 6:9-11 is a keen reminder of what it means to have a new identity. Here Paul writes,

> *Or do you not know that the unrighteous will not inherit the kingdom of God? Do not be deceived: neither the sexually immoral, nor idolaters, nor adulterers, nor men who practice homosexuality, nor thieves, nor the greedy, nor drunkards, nor revilers, nor swindlers will inherit the kingdom of God. And such were some of you. But you were washed, you were sanctified, you were justified in the name of the Lord Jesus Christ and by the Spirit of our God.*

If your behavior is no different from the unsaved world, you may not be among the redeemed. Salvation is always evidenced by progress toward godly living. Instead of being described by your sinfulness, as a believer you ought to be described by your growing holiness. The life of sin must be your "used to be" and not your now. Be assured that grace and forgiveness is available in Christ. You need not live in shame and under condemnation but can find his total cleansing (1 John 1:9).

Earlier we stated that those who haven't gained victory over pornography are not ready for ministry. The same is true for those who have not gained victory over same sex attraction. Before you can serve in church leadership, your character must be defined by a long record of victory over sexual temptation.

Application Questions or Activities

1. If you are single, how effectively are you resisting the urge to waste your singleness?

2. Consider your current relationships with the opposite sex. Where have you been maintaining healthy boundaries? Where have you let your guard down? Are there any relationships that have already gone too far and need to be cut off immediately?

3. Consider your ministry practices with the opposite sex. Where have you placed healthy boundaries? What new boundaries do you need to put in place?

4. What do you need to confess and repent of to your spouse this evening?

5. How healthy is your relationship with your children? How much time are you spending with your children? When have you unduly exasperated them? When have you enabled them to continue sinning against you, the rest of the family, and God? What sin and failure do you need to confess to your children today?

6. Honestly assess the current condition of your marriage. Ask your spouse their thoughts on the condition of your marriage and your family. Is it healthy or is there a danger of it imploding, or is there a danger of you seeking comfort outside of your marriage? Is it time to seek help?

Chapter 6: You and Your Resources

"Every financial transaction reveals our heart by presenting an opportunity to worship Jesus and serve his kingdom, or worship ourselves and serve our own lesser kingdom. All of us, "haves" and "have nots" alike, will use our money to serve the priorities of the god we worship."[47]

We began our study on how to manage our household by first looking at why we should be good managers. We also talked about managing ourselves, managing our marriage, managing our children, and managing our other relationships. We talked about how to guard our household by guarding ourselves from the destructive sources that seek to tear us and our household apart. Part of managing our household well includes the management of our resources.

How Rich Are You?

How rich are you? How much grace has God poured out into your life? Don't compare yourself to other people. Don't think of it in terms of comparing your country with other nations of the world. We will always find people who have more than we have. That kind of comparison will only leave us discouraged and wishing we would have more.

Think of your wealth from God's viewpoint. In his eyes, how rich are you? What has he given you? The following questions can be used as calculator of your wealth:

- How much grace has God given you? What has he given you through his work of redemption? (See Eph. 1:3-14).

---

[47] Jamie Monson, *Money: God or Gift,* (2014: Seattle, WA, The Money Mission), 18.

- What about your family heritage? What have you gained from being connected to your family?

- Who has the Lord given you to be your wife?

- How many children do you have?

- How much time do you have? Each day, week, and year?

- How much health and energy do you have?

- What spiritual gifts has the Spirit given you with which to serve him and others? What are they?

- How much education has he allowed you to obtain?

- What abilities & skills has God given you that allow you to take care of yourself and your family?

- What kind of career or job do you have that allows you to pay for the expenses of life?

- How many friends do you have? Name them.

- How many of those friends can you call on to help you when you are in trouble or face a crisis? Name them.

- How much money has he blessed you with?

- What kind of transportation do you have?

Your Money

Stewardship Principles

As you seek to manage the resources God has given you, here are five basic stewardship principles that will guide your thinking. The first principle is that God is the source of all things. *For by him all things were created, in heaven and on earth, visible and invisible, whether thrones or dominions or ruler or authorities — all things were created through him and for him* (Colossians 1:16). He is even the source of our ability to create or earn wealth. *Beware lest you say in your heart, 'My power and the might of my hand have gotten me this wealth. You shall remember the Lord your God, for it is he who gives you the power to get wealth*

(Deuteronomy 8:17-18).

The second principle states that God owns everything. He owns both heaven and earth. In one of his prayers, David said,

> *Blessed are you, O LORD, the God of Israel our father, forever and ever. Yours, O LORD, is the greatness and the power and the glory and the victory and the majesty, for all that is in the heavens and in the earth is yours. Yours is the kingdom, O LORD, and you are exalted as head above all. Both riches and honor come from you, and you rule over all. In your hand are power and might, and in your hand it is to make great and to give strength to all. And now we thank you, our God, and praise your glorious name.* (1 Chronicles 29:10-13).

In Psalm 24:1-2 he adds, *The earth is the Lord's and the fullness thereof, the world and those who dwell therein, for he has founded it upon the seas and established it upon the rivers.*

While we like to put our names on the things we own, God is the one who owns all the wealth of the earth. *Both riches and honor come from you, and you rule over all* (1 Chronicles 29:12). The prophet Haggai wrote, *The silver is mine, and the gold is mine, declares the Lord of hosts* (Haggai 2:8).

God owns all the living creatures on the earth. In Psalm 50:10-11 he says, *For every beast of the forest is mine, and the cattle on a thousand hills. I know all the birds of the hills, and all that moves in the field is mine.* God also owns and controls all the times and seasons. Daniel wrote, *Blessed be the name of God forever and ever, to whom belongs wisdom and might. He changes the times and seasons* (Daniel 2:20-21). He owns all leadership. In the prayer of David mentioned above, David says, *In your hand are power and might and in your hand it is to make great and to give strength to all* (1 Chronicles 29:12). Daniel added, *He removes kings and sets up kings* (Daniel 2:21).

God owns everything! Everything you put your name on belongs to God. Where you live, what you wear, what you eat, the money you have saved, the animals you own, all belong to God. We may cling to what we have, but it really does not belong to us. It belongs to God.

The third principle of stewardship is that God desires contentment. We need to remember that we brought nothing into this world, and we can take nothing out of it (1 Timothy 6:6-7). As we journey through life, we need to trust God to provide for us. Paul wrote, *But if we have food and clothing, with these we will be content* (1 Timothy 6:8). Will we really? Are they enough? Here is what Jesus said,

> *Therefore I tell you, do not be anxious about your life, what you will eat or what you will drink, nor about your body, what you will put on. Is not life more than food, and the body more than clothing? Look at the birds of the air: they neither sow nor reap nor gather into barns, and yet your heavenly Father feeds them. Are you not of more value than they? And which of you by being anxious can add a single hour to his span of life? And why are you anxious about clothing? Consider the lilies of the field, how they grow: they neither toil nor spin, yet I tell you, even Solomon in all his glory was not arrayed like one of these. But if God so clothes the grass of the field, which today is alive and tomorrow is thrown into the oven, will he not much more clothe you, O you of little faith?* (Matthew 6:25-30).

God knows exactly what you, your family, and your church needs. He knows!

The Bible also teaches us that craving for more leads us away from dependence on God. Paul wrote,

> *But those who desire to be rich fall into temptation, into a snare, into many senseless and harmful desires that plunge people into ruin and destruction. For the love of money is a root of all kinds of evils. It is through this craving that some have wandered away from the faith and pierced themselves with many pangs* (1 Timothy 6:9-10).

Craving things leads to idolatry where our money and our possessions take a more prominent place than God. In fact, they will crowd God out of our life. But the sad truth is this, we will find they do not satisfy. Living for more always leads us to wanting more. Our craving becomes insatiable. This is the reason Paul told Timothy than a lover of money could not be an elder (1 Timothy 3:3). He told Titus that someone greedy for more would also be disqualified from eldership (Titus 1:7). Perhaps we should all regularly incorporate Proverbs 30:7-9 in our prayers:

Two things I ask of you; deny them not to me before I die: Remove far from me falsehood and lying; give me neither poverty nor riches; feed me with the food that is needful for me, lest I be full and deny you and say, "Who is the LORD?" or lest I be poor and steal and profane the name of my God.

The fourth principle of stewardship that should guide our thinking and decision making is that God expects accountability. Matthew records a lengthy parable of Jesus about the kingdom of heaven that is worth repeating here.

For it will be like a man going on a journey, who called his servants and entrusted to them his property. To one he gave five talents, to another two, to another one, to each according to his ability. Then he went away. He who had received the five talents went at once and traded with them, and he made five talents more. So also he who had the two talents made two talents more. But he who had received the one talent went and dug in the ground and hid his master's money. Now after a long time the master of those servants came and settled accounts with them. And he who had received the five talents came forward, bringing five talents more, saying, 'Master, you delivered to me five talents; here I have made five talents more.' His master said to him, 'Well done, good and faithful servant. You have been faithful over a little; I will set you over much. Enter into the joy of your master.' And he also who had the two talents came forward, saying, 'Master, you delivered to me two talents; here I have made two talents more.' His master said to him, 'Well done, good and faithful servant. You have been faithful over a little; I will set you over much. Enter into the joy of your master.' He also who had received the one talent came forward, saying, 'Master, I knew you to be a hard man, reaping where you did not sow, and gathering where you scattered no seed, so I was afraid, and I went and hid your talent in the ground. Here you have what is yours.' But his master answered him, 'You wicked and slothful servant! You knew that I reap where I have not sowed and gather where I scattered no seed? Then you ought to have invested my money with the bankers, and at my coming I should have received what was my own with interest. So take the talent from him and give it to him who has the ten talents. For to everyone who has will more be given, and he will have an abundance. But from the one who has not, even what he has will be taken away. And cast the worthless servant into the outer darkness. In that place there will be weeping and gnashing of teeth (Matthew 25:14-30).

God will hold us accountable as to how we used the wealth that he entrusted to us. This includes our time, our measure of health, our possessions, our relationships, and the wealth we have accumulated. What will not be important is the amount we were entrusted with, but how we used it to participate in the building of his kingdom.

What we do with the amount God has currently entrusted to us will also have an impact on future entrustments from God. Jesus said,

One who is faithful in a very little is also faithful in much, and one who is dishonest in a very little is also dishonest in much. If then you have not been faithful in the unrighteous wealth, who will entrust to you true riches? And if you have not been faithful in that which is

another's, who will give you that which is your own? (Luke 16:10-12).

If God cannot trust us with a little, how can he trust us with more? There are times we pray that God would pour out his abundance on us, but could it be that one of the reasons we don't see our prayer answered is because we have not been faithful stewards of what he has already entrusted to us?

The fifth principle of stewardship we need to remember is that God will not compete with money. Jesus made this very clear when he said, *No servant can serve two masters, for either he will hate the one and love the other; or he will be devoted to the one and despise the other. You cannot serve God and money* (Luke 16:13).

How can we tell if we are serving money? There are two ways. First, we continually scheme and try to get more. Our thoughts are filled with the "what if" and the "if only." What if we won the lottery? What if someone gave us a huge amount of money? If only we had more? If we did this or that, we could get more.

Continually complaining about the lack of money is the second way we can tell we are serving money. When we complain, we are saying that God has not provided for us. He has not kept his promises. It is the same as saying he cannot be fully trusted to take care of us; therefore we will take this task on our own shoulders to make up for his deficiency. That is a very serious statement! If you want to know how serious this is, read through the book of Numbers where you will discover God's response to the continual complaints of the people of Israel as they spent time under God's care in the Sinai wilderness. You would not wish God's reaction on yourself or anyone else!

Budgeting Principles

To help you financially manage your household well, you need a plan. That plan is called a budget. Some see a budget as a method of worrying before you spend as well as afterwards. It has been called an orderly, time-consuming and methodical way to discover there is not enough money to go around. It has also been labelled as an attempt to live below your yearnings.

A budget is a useful tool to help us live out our values and reach our financial goals. It helps us set out our priorities and gives us a clear picture of what is possible with the income that is currently available.

There are a lot of reasons people do not budget. For some it is a perceived loss of freedom. They feel they must account for the money they spend and they have never had to do that before. Some people believe ignorance is bliss. They prefer not to know how bad their financial situation is. For others it is a lack of discipline. It doesn't make sense to take the time to develop a budget if they have no intention of living according to it. For some it is simple procrastination. It takes work to make a budget and sometimes it is easier to ignore doing it. Others see budgeting as a tool only poor people need.

Whatever the viewpoint, there are significant benefits to budgeting. A budget provides an accurate picture of your finances. It helps you determine what is important. A budget also makes you a smarter consumer because it forces you to think whether you are making the best possible purchase. A budget is a tool to help you control your money so that your lack of money does not control you.

Laying a Foundation for Writing a Budget

One of the most common sources of marital conflict is money. However, there are some things you can do before writing and keeping a budget that will lessen some of the tension surrounding money.

First, we will never be able to effectively write a budget, much less maintain a stewardship plan until we begin to see our money in the context of God's vision for our marriage. As a reminder, family is primarily designed by God to be a school of discipleship. It is an instrument of sanctification in our lives. Through it we are to reflect his glory to each other and those around us. Through our families we illustrate to others how he loves his children in the way that we love each other as husband and wife. How we manage our money is one of the ways in which we either reveal or hinder that vision.

Second, prayerfully determine how God has specifically called your family to carry out that vision. Are you called to a ministry of hospitality? Are you called to a career that requires significant and expensive education and training? Are you called to give generously to the needy? Are you called to self-supporting mission work? Are you called to invest in others' futures? Are you called to have a large family? One thing we know from the start: you are not called to use your money for selfish purposes. Your money is but one resource that God provides for you that you might be able to accomplish that vision in your marriage.

The third principle is once you've prayerfully established a godly vision for you family, and by extension your money, establish priorities. For example, what is more important?

- Giving to the work of the Lord first, or giving what might be left over after everything else is paid for?
- Giving to those in need or saving money?
- Setting aside money for later in life or maintaining a higher standard of living, now?
- Taking an annual vacation or paying back what you owe other people?

- Continuing your education or getting a larger house?

As you strive to determine your family's vision and priorities, do not forsake the joy that comes from the gifts God has given you. Your money is a blessing, provided by God, meant to be enjoyed. It's okay to spend a reasonable amount of your money on the personal enrichment and the comfort of your family to the degree that you can afford it without sacrificing your primary vision.

Fourth, you may need to spend some time tracking your spending before you begin writing a budget. Keep your receipts or write down in a spending journal how much you spend on groceries, fuel, clothing, recreation, etc. for a month. You will almost certainly be surprised at how much you spend in each category. This will help you avoid putting unrealistic funds in each category.

Writing a Budget

What should be included in a budget? The list below gives you an idea of the kinds of things to include. Not everything on this list will apply to you and your situation, but it serves as an example of what to consider when making a budget.

- Giving to the Lord and others
- Groceries
- Clothing
- House payments or rent
- Property taxes
- Other taxes
- House insurance
- Natural gas
- Electricity

- Water & sewer
- Cell phones
- Internet/TV
- Car payments
- Car insurance
- Vehicle fuel
- Vehicle maintenance
- Health costs
- Gifts (Christmas, birthdays, anniversary, weddings)
- Vacation costs
- Entertainment/hobbies/sports
- Life insurance
- Retirement savings
- Savings for emergencies or new purchases
- Emergency funds
- Individual allowances for incidentals
- Miscellaneous

How do you make a budget? The first step is to sit down with your wife and a favorite beverage and do this together. Be prepared that this exercise may cause some tension between you. Be sure to listen to her and not make judgement statements to each other or attack each other for the problems and misunderstandings you will be sure to discover.

Second, under each of these categories write the monthly amount you spend (refer to your receipts or spending journal). Add up the total and compare it to your income. It might be scary, but you will quickly discover how you are doing.

Most people will need to make some adjustments to the numbers to get them to match their income. You will also have to work through differing ideas about what is important. You may not agree on every financial decision, but you need to specifically talk about what is important so that you can work together on keeping to the budget.

Most of us will also have to set up some guidelines that will be followed to make the budget work. These may include decisions to not use credit cards to extend your buying power. You may need to set a limit on how much money each of you can spend without first asking the other. You may want to give each other a small monthly allowance to spend without accountability. You may need to commit yourselves to stop going to the shopping mall as a form of entertainment where you will be attracted to what you see and inevitably spend money you never intended on things you don't need.

Giving Principles

Giving should be a part of every believer's financial plan. In fact, our giving makes a significant statement about what is important to us. Giving reveals where our heart is. Jesus said,

> *Do not lay up for yourselves treasures on earth, where moth and rust destroy and where thieves break in and steal, but lay up for yourselves treasures in heaven, where neither moth nor rust destroys and where thieves do not break in and steal. For where your treasure is, there your heart will be also* (Matthew 6:19-21).

Giving is also an act that expresses our dependence on God. In Luke 6:38, Jesus said, *Give, and it will be given to you. Good measure, pressed down, shaken together, running over, will be put into your lap. For the measure you use it will be measured back to you.* Paul made this promise to the Philippian believers in response to their generous gift to his ministry:

> *I am well supplied, having received from Epaphroditus the gifts you*

sent, a fragrant offering, a sacrifice acceptable and pleasing to God. And my God will supply every need of yours according to his riches in glory in Christ Jesus (Philippians 4:18-19).

When giving is the first thing we do with a portion of our income, we are making a statement that we trust the Lord for the need or for the deficit we may find ourselves in due to our gift. But we can be assured that our giving will not leave us in need. Paul wrote,

> *And God is able to make all grace abound to you, so that having all sufficiency in all things at all times, you may abound in every good work. As it is written, "He has distributed freely, he has given to the poor; his righteousness endures forever." He who supplies seed to the sower and bread for food will supply and multiply your seed for sowing and increase the harvest of your righteousness. You will be enriched in every way for all your generosity, which through us will produce thanksgiving to God* (2 Corinthians 9:8-11).

We also need to remember that while our giving should primarily be done at the place we are being spiritually fed (Galatians 6:6; 1 Corinthians 9:13-14), our giving is not to a church or ministry, but to God. To not give to him is to rob him (Malachi 3:8, 10)!

While there is much debate on the amount we are to give, it seems that the New Testament teaches that our giving should be at least ten percent. Jesus told the religious leaders of his day, *Woe to you, scribes and Pharisees, hypocrites! For you tithe mint and dill and cumin, and have neglected the weightier matters of the law: justice and mercy and faithfulness. These you ought to have done without neglecting the others* (Matthew 23:23). The Pharisees were so careful in following the law that required them to give a tenth of all that was produced that they paid the tithe even from the smallest garden crops. Jesus does not say they were wrong in this, but that they should do this without neglecting the far more important matters. In saying this,

Jesus endorsed the law of tithing or of giving at least ten percent. Paul pushed this further and told the Corinthian church, *Whoever sows sparingly will also reap sparingly, and whoever sows bountifully will also reap bountifully. Each one must give as he has decided in his heart, not reluctantly or under compulsion, for God loves a cheerful giver* (2 Corinthians 9:6-7).

Whatever amount you decide to give, it is an expression of worship that says, "God owns everything, even what I hold in my hand, and I will lay a generous portion at his feet as an act of worship, acknowledging his greatness and my absolute dependence on him and trust in him."

Your Time

One of the greatest resources we have is time. Sometimes we feel we do not have enough and other times we feel we have too much. The truth is, we all have the same amount of time. We all have 168 hours each week, 24 hours each day, and 60 minutes each hour. The problem is often not how much time we have, but how we manage our time.

Paul instructs us to *Look carefully then how you walk, not as unwise but as wise, making the best use of the time, because the days are evil* (Ephesians 5:15-16). Fifteen hundred years earlier Moses asked God to help us *to number our days that we may get a heart of wisdom* (Psalm 90:12).

We all find ourselves in different seasons of life. Each season has its own set of demands and responsibilities. Since we only have so much time and energy each week, we need to be sure to make the best use of it, keeping all things in balance.

Our planning and use of time must always be governed by the will of God. James said,

> *Come now, you who say, "Today or tomorrow we will go into such and*

such a town and spend a year there and trade and make a profit"—
yet you do not know what tomorrow will bring. What is your life? For
you are a mist that appears for a little time and then vanishes. Instead
you ought to say, "If the Lord wills, we will live and do this or that."
James 4:13-15).

To plan our lives and schedule without God is foolish. We do
not know what tomorrow will bring. We do not know how long
we will live. Therefore, our time management must begin with an
ongoing surrender to his sovereignty.

To plan our time and schedule without making room for
prayer and the study of the Word will mean we lose the daily
nourishment that feeds our trust in God and his promises. To not
plan to pray is usually to not pray. To not pray is arrogance that
says to God, "I got this. I do not need you. I can handle today and
all it will bring." Or it is faithlessness that says of God, "You can't
or won't do anything about it, anyway. Why bother to ask?"

To plan our time and schedule without flexibility could mean
we miss opportunities to do good to others. We need to be flexible
enough to drop what we are doing to meet the needs of others in
our household and community. This flexibility allows for those
blessed interruptions where the Spirit wants to use us to meet a
need, be an encouragement, listen to a broken heart, or provide
an extra set of hands.

To plan our time and schedule only around our "to do" list,
forgetting the people God has entrusted to our care, is to be
irresponsible in the assignment God has given us. Each person
who enters our household, whether by marriage, by birth, or by
friendship, is an assignment from the Lord to love and care for
them as he has done for us. This assignment takes time. Lots of
time. It is not that we schedule people into certain time slots, but
it is that we make room in our planning for the times these people

need our attention and care. A schedule that is too tight will only lead us to resent the interruptions and eventually the people who interrupt.

In his book, *The Habits of Grace,* David Mathis gives four lessons in fruitful time management.[48] Consider our calling. What has God called us to do today? What does he want our life to be about right now? We may have plans for the future, but what is our station and calling during this season of our life?

Plan the big pieces. What are the key priorities that make up our calling? What are the big things that need to be planned with intentionality? There are lots of little things we do every day, but they will tend to crowd out the big things if we put the little things first.

Third, we need to make the most of our mornings. Many studies have shown how important it is to use the first hours of the day to fulfil the most important parts of our calling. In the morning we are usually our sharpest and have the greatest amount of energy. Early in the morning we are also less likely to be interrupted and distracted. When the most important thing in our day is to be reconnected to Jesus and his Word, we are more likely to put that at the beginning of our day. When we leave that to chance, we are more likely to leave it behind and end our day without that connection.

Create flexibility in our schedule for meeting the needs of others in our household and community. Since our calling is to live for the glory of God, displaying him in all we do and say, God will bring people across our path so they experience a taste of his grace and love. We need to be disciplined enough to get our work done, yet flexible enough to love others in those unplanned times. Matthis writes,

---

[48] Mathis, David, *Habits of Grace*, Crossway, 2016, 215-218.

The greatest joys come not from time squandered, hoarded, or selfishly spent, but from self-sacrificial love for others to the glory of God, when we pour out our time and energy for the good of others, and find our joy in theirs.[49]

We need to reserve space in our schedule for time in the Word, prayer, reading theological and inspirational texts and sitting under others' teaching. But we also need time to just rest. Just as our spiritual selves needs rest, so to our physical bodies. Edward Welch often refers to mankind as "embodied souls."[50] He means among other things that the physical and spiritual are so intricately intertwined that the health or lack thereof of one will always affect the other. Spiritual fatigue will somehow have physiological symptoms. Physiological issues such as illness, insomnia, or serious injury, will often make it harder for us to believe and live out the gospel promises that we so cherish and teach others to cherish.

Your Spiritual Gifts

Managing your household well includes managing and developing the gifts and abilities God has given you. A spiritual gift is a special ability given to believers by the Holy Spirit so they effectively serve in the ministry of building up and maturing the body of Christ. They differ from natural talents in that natural talents are given to us at birth from God through the genetic inheritance we receive from our parents. Spiritual gifts are given to us at our new birth and prepare us for ministry within the Body of Christ. However, our spiritual gifts can be closely tied with our God-given personality and talents.

---

[49] Mathis, 218.

[50] Edward T. Welch, "The Psychological does not Exist," Christian Counseling and Education Foundation, Blogpost last modified: May 29th, 2014, https://www.ccef.org/psychological-does-not-exist/.

The Bible outlines some basic things about spiritual gifts. Here is a list of passages and what we can see in each one:

- 1 Peter 4:10-11
    - Every believer has at least one spiritual gift.
    - Each one is to use his/her gifts to serve.
    - Each one is to be faithful.
- 1 Corinthians 12:7
    - Every believer has a spiritual gift.
    - Gifts are given for the common good of the church family.
- 1 Corinthians 12:11
    - We cannot choose our gifts. They are given as God determines.
- 1 Corinthians 13:1-3
    - Gifts used without love do not accomplish God's intended purposes.
- Romans 12:3-8
    - We each have a unique function in the Body of Christ.
    - We are not independent of each other. We belong to each other, and we need each other.
    - We have differing gifts and we are to use them.

While the Bible does not give us a detailed definition of each gift, there have been many different definitions attached to them. The Bible simply gives us lists of gifts. Because no two biblical list of gifts is identical, it would seem to suggest that the biblical lists are illustrative rather than exhaustive.

How do we discover which gift or gifts the Holy Spirit has given to us? There are various spiritual gift inventories available, but spiritual gifts are best discovered in the context of serving. It is best done in the context of people who can observe you in ministry.

First, you need to ask yourself: What is it I like doing? What is it that gets me excited and enthusiastic? Second, you need to ask others what they see you as being good at? How have they seen the Holy Spirit at work through you? Third, you simply need to get involved in ministry. As you serve the Lord and others you will, by the Spirit, naturally do what he has gifted you to do.

As you invest in the lives of others and use your spiritual gifts, there are some things to remember. Each person's gifts are valuable and necessary. Even though you may only see yourself as one among many, your spiritual gifts are necessary to the health and growth of the Body of Christ. All are valuable and necessary. When we sit back and become only church attendees, and let others serve us, we miss out on the joy of fulfilment that comes when we are doing what the Lord has called us to do.

The church is not somebody else. If you are a believer, the church is you. When you criticize the church for not doing something the way you think it should be done, you are not just talking about others, you are talking about yourself. If you only expect to be served by others in the church, you have caused the church to become dysfunctional. When you see a need in the church you can either become critical of what others are not doing, or you can begin to invest your gifts and abilities into bringing about solutions. It is up to you to choose to be part of the problem or part of the solution.

Not everyone in the church family will be motivated to respond to needs and opportunities in the same way. Our spiritual gifts define what we are to be doing in response to the needs of others. What you are to do and what another person is to do may be very different because your gifts are very different. Someone with the gift of prophecy might speak to bring conviction to a sinning believer. The person with the gift of teaching might help them find the biblical application that will bring growth. The gift of mercy will support and love and protect the sinner, helping them get through the problem. The gift of intercession will pray diligently for the sinner. Each one will respond to the need, bringing their unique contribution to the need. Don't be critical of how others serve. Their gifts are just as important as yours. Allow each other freedom to be all that God has called them to be.

Spiritual gifts exercised without love cause more hurt than help. Every strength pushed to its extreme becomes a weakness. When we push our way of doing things, as right as it may be, we alienate ourselves from the body rather than become a part of encouraging it. To help us understand how spiritual gifts are to be used, 1 Corinthians 13 is wedged between Chapters 12 (a description of how the body functions) and Chapter 14 (instructions for solving spiritual gift problems). We tend to relegate 1 Corinthians 13 to weddings, but the context suggests that it is all about gift ministry in the church. Without love, our gifts become empty and useless. But as we minister in love, we will make an eternal difference.

Our spiritual gifts were given to be used in the care of others. This means we need to intentionally find place where we can use the gifts God has given so that others in our household and the household of God receive his benefit and blessing.

Managing our household includes managing our resources of money, time, and spiritual giftedness. How is your management of these things?

<u>Application Questions or Activities</u>

1. How would you measure your godliness in financial matters? Use the chart below for your evaluation.

Godliness in Financial Matters

a. One who displays godliness in financial matters.

> *... not a lover of money* (1 Tim. 3:3)
>
> *... not pursuing dishonest gain* (Titus 1:7)
>
> *... not greedy for money, but eager to serve* (1 Peter 5:2)

An elder's attention must not be riveted on money. His decisions must not be dictated only by financial concerns. He must be generous and set an example in giving, not pursuing his ministry for personal gain.

Weak				**Strong**
1	2	3	4	5

b. One who desires to do good and not evil.

> *... one who loves what is good* (Titus 1:8)

An elder must be one who is ready to do what is beneficial for others. He must be a person whose actions show that he desires to reflect God's goodness in all his choices and attitudes. He must keep the best interests of others in mind.

Weak				**Strong**
1	2	3	4	5

c. One whose life is set apart for God.

> *... holy* (Titus 1:8)

An elder must have an earnest desire to live a life that is pleasing to God. He must place a high priority on spiritual growth. His life must demonstrate that his heart is centered on God and not on worldly fortune.

Weak				**Strong**
1	2	3	4	5

2. As you review the qualities outlined above how do you measure up? Has weakness in any of these areas disqualified you from leadership at this time? Where do you need to keep growing? What do you need to do to progress toward godliness in these areas? What are you going to do?

3. Take some time to make a list of your resources. If you are married, do this with your wife. On your list, be sure to include the following from pages 145-146:
    a) How much grace has God given you? What has he given you in redeeming you? (See Ephesians 1:3-14).
    b) What about your family heritage? What have you gained from being connected to your family?
    c) Who has the Lord given to you to be your wife?
    d) How many children do you have?
    e) How much time do you have? Each day, week, and year?
    f) How much health and energy do you have?
    g) What spiritual gifts has the Spirit given you with which to serve him and others? What are they?
    h) How much education has he allowed you to obtain?
    i) What abilities and skills has God given you that allow you to take care of yourself and your family?
    j) What kind of career or job do you have that allows you to pay for the expenses of life?
    k) How many friends do you have? Name them.
    l) How many of those friends can you call on to help you when you are in trouble or face a crisis? Name them.
    m) How much money has he blessed you with?
    n) What kind of transportation do you have?

4. Since managing your household well includes the management of the resources God has blessed you with, how are you doing? Do you recognize that you are a steward of all you have been given? Do you realize that you will stand before your Master to give an account of what you have done with what hehas entrusted to you? What areas of your life have you failed to acknowledge his Lordship?

5. If you do not already have a budget, set aside some time to work on this with your wife. Be careful to be patient, to listen to her ideas and concerns, and to gently lead your household in setting a direction that will please the Lord.

6. What do other people say about your ministry investments? What do they see as your contribution to the life and ministry of the church? Which of the spiritual gifts do they see at work through your life as you serve the Lord?

Chapter 7: You and Your Church

What is the Church?

We have spoken in some detail about how and why God reveals himself and works out his redemptive plan in family, but most who are reading this book are now, or aspire to be, elders, pastors, and ministry leaders in the context of a local congregation. As such, we are called to lead not only our family, but the church. For elders and pastors, not only do we manage our household well for the well-being of our family and its reputation, but we also manage our households for the well-being and reputation of the church. Nothing is more damaging to a congregation than the fall of one or more of its leaders.

There are but two institutions designed and preserved by God in Scripture: the family and the church. It is here in the context of these two institutions that God choses to reveal his glory, majesty, grace, and mercy. They are the primary conduits through which his redemption flows into the lives of his children, transforming our hearts from a heart of stone to a heart of flesh (Ezekiel 36:26).

To help us with our task we need to know what the church is, what it is to look like and what it is to be doing. To help us with this, Peter provides us with a beautiful, descriptive, and concise illustration of the church in 1 Peter 2:1-10:

> *So put away all malice and all deceit and hypocrisy and envy and all slander. Like newborn infants, long for the pure spiritual milk, that by it you may grow up into salvation — if indeed you have tasted that the Lord is good. As you come to him, a living stone rejected by men but in the sight of God chosen and precious, you yourselves like living stones are being built up as a spiritual house, to be a holy priesthood, to offer spiritual sacrifices acceptable to God through Jesus Christ. For it stands in Scripture: "Behold, I am laying in Zion a stone, a*

cornerstone chosen and precious, and whoever believes in him will not be put to shame." So the honor is for you who believe, but for those who do not believe, "The stone that the builders rejected has become the cornerstone," and "A stone of stumbling, and a rock of offense."

They stumble because they disobey the word, as they were destined to do. But you are a chosen race, a royal priesthood, a holy nation, a people for his own possession, that you may proclaim the excellencies of him who called you out of darkness into his marvelous light. Once you were not a people, but now you are God's people; once you had not received mercy, but now you have received mercy.

In this passage, Peter teaches us at least three things about the body of Christ. First, we are a people of one origin. We are told to *put away all malice and all deceit, and hypocrisy and envy and slander.* These are the things that identify where we have come from. They were what flowed out of our hearts as rancid evidence of our sinful character and lack of integrity. We are to forsake our old tendencies in exchange for living as a *holy priesthood, to offer spiritual sacrifices acceptable to God through Jesus Christ.*

Further, Peter exhorts us to, *like newborn infants, long for spiritual milk, that by it you grow up into salvation.* In other words, we once did not long for the precious and lifegiving truths of the gospel. Instead, we passionately pursued any number of poisonous and deadly false messiahs including pleasures of the flesh and anti-gospel ideologies. But now we cling to, rest in, find comfort in and rejoice over the fact that we each *like living stones are being built up as a spiritual house, to be a holy priesthood, to offer spiritual sacrifices acceptable to God through Jesus Christ.* We were once spiritually dead but are now alive in Christ (Ephesians 2:1-10).

Peter not only teaches us that we are of one origin, but he also teaches us that we are built on one foundation. The living stones, being built up as a spiritual house, are built on the solid foundation of the stone being laid in Zion. He describes it as *a cornerstone chosen and precious and whoever believes in him will not be put to shame.* Peter is quoting from Isaiah 28:16 and connects it to Psalm 118:22-23 to show us that Jesus, in fulfillment of prophecy, is the foundation of the church. This picture is made even more explicit in Ephesians 2:19-22:

> *So then you are no longer strangers and aliens, but you are fellow citizens with the saints and members of the household of God, built on the foundation of the apostles and prophets, Christ Jesus himself being the cornerstone, in whom the whole structure, being joined together, grows into a holy temple in the Lord. In him you also are being built together into a dwelling place for God by the Spirit.*

Peter concludes with an awe-inspiring anthem of what we are as these living stones:

> *But you are a chosen race, a royal priesthood, a holy nation, a people for his own possession, that you may proclaim the excellencies of him who called you out of darkness into his marvelous light. Once you were not a people, but now you are God's people; once you had not received mercy, but now you have received mercy* (1 Peter 2: 9-10).

In other words, we are a people of one origin, built on one foundation, and are a people of one bond. As the church we are chosen by God to be both royalty (leaders) and priests (intercessors between God and the world)! Through the person and work of Christ, we are declared holy (though we do not always act as such). Through that same person and work of Christ, we are God's people. Our purpose is to proclaim his glorious character and deeds to the nations because hehas called us out of the darkness and into his marvelous light! And because all of this has happened in him, and through him, and because of him, we are now his people who have received mercy!

When we as elders and pastors invite people to become members of and participate in the body of Christ, we are inviting them to become a part of nothing less than this marvelous family! It is this family that we are called to care for. It is this family that we are called to lead. Is it any wonder that Paul tells Timothy that *the elders who rule well should be considered worthy of a double honor, especially those who labor in preaching and teaching* (1 Tim. 5:17)?

Our Connection to the Church

We have looked at what it means to manage our own lives, our marriages, our children, and our resources. We have also talked about guarding our household by guarding our own hearts and lives. But there is one more area we want to consider. We are leaders in our homes and we are leaders in the church. But how do we connect our household to the church?

Consider what Paul wrote in Ephesians 1:1-14:

Paul, an apostle of Christ Jesus by the will of God, To the saints who are in Ephesus, and are faithful in Christ Jesus: Grace to you and peace from God our Father and the Lord Jesus Christ.

Blessed be the God and Father of our Lord Jesus Christ, who has blessed us in Christ with every spiritual blessing in the heavenly places, even as he chose us in him before the foundation of the world, that we should be holy and blameless before him. In love he predestined us for adoption to himself as sons through Jesus Christ, according to the purpose of his will, to the praise of his glorious grace, with which he has blessed us in the Beloved. In him we have redemption through his blood, the forgiveness of our trespasses, according to the riches of his grace, which he lavished upon us, in all wisdom and insight making known to us the mystery of his will, according to his purpose, which he set forth in Christ as a plan for the fullness of time, to unite all things in him, things in heaven and things on earth.

> *In him we have obtained an inheritance, having been predestined according to the purpose of him who works all things according to the counsel of his will, so that we who were the first to hope in Christ might be to the praise of his glory. In him you also, when you heard the word of truth, the gospel of your salvation, and believed in him, were sealed with the promised Holy Spirit, who is the guarantee of our inheritance until we acquire possession of it, to the praise of his glory.*

As Paul begins this great letter, notice that he writes to *the saints who are in Ephesus*. This is the church of Ephesus. This is the community of believers who have been redeemed by the grace of God. These are the people who have surrendered to the call of God and now enjoy the blessings of redemption.

Notice the wonderful list of blessings that are ours in Christ Jesus:

- In eternity past God chose us to be holy and blameless (1:4).
- In eternity past God ordained or appointed us to be adopted as sons or heirs of all the blessings of eternity (1:5).
- We have been ransomed from captivity and slavery to our sins and have been given the forgiveness of sin by Christ's atoning sacrifice (1:7).
- Because we have been adopted as sons into God's family, we have an inheritance or an allotted portion of the eternal blessings of God (1:11).
- The Holy Spirit has been given as a seal or down payment of what is to come in the eternal kingdom of God (1:13).

So how does the church fit into all of this? What has this got to do with managing our household well?

If you read on in Ephesians you will find that chapter 2 tells us of the journey we have taken into God's grace and the resulting relationship we have not only with Christ, but with one another. When we get to verse 2:19-22 we read,

> *So then you are no longer strangers and aliens, but you are fellow citizens with the saints and members of the household of God, built on the foundation of the apostles and prophets, Christ Jesus himself being the cornerstone, in whom the whole structure, being joined together, grows into a holy temple in the Lord. In him you also are being built together into a dwelling place for God by the Spirit.*

Did you notice the phrase *members of the household of God?* Believers are joined together into the household of God or the family of God. We are connected to one another in this great family. We have been adopted in and now have a place and an inheritance in God's household.

While the household of God will extend into eternity, it finds expression here on earth in local churches. It finds expression in the gatherings of believers that are scattered all over this country and around the world. Some meet in great cathedrals. Others meet under trees or in caves. The place of worship or the size of the church does not matter. But what does matter is that it is the family of God.

The Church as a Family of Families

How does that impact us as family leaders? We need to view the local church as an extended family, not just a group to join and in which to serve. In 1 Timothy 3:15 Paul calls the local church the *household of God*. If it is that, we must place a high priority on our involvement in the local church and must guard against other community and social organizations taking priority.

Members of the local church are to be viewed as family members and be treated with similar respect and support as one would show his own immediate family. In 1 Tim. 5:1-2 Paul calls us to view and treat older men as fathers, older women as mothers, younger men as brothers and younger women as sisters.

As we have been learning, only the heads of households who do a good job of managing their own immediate family are qualified to help lead the extended family, the local church (1 Tim. 3:4-5; Titus 1:6).

Older women are to help the younger women in building godly homes, teaching them how to love their husbands and children, how to respond to their husbands, and how to manage their home responsibilities. (Titus 2:3-5)

Paul goes on in 1 Timothy 5:3-16 to tell us that our commitment to the local church as an extended family has implications for those older members who are not able to provide for themselves. Widows who have served both households (their individual family and the church family) are to be financially supported if their immediate families cannot support them.

Connecting Your Family to the Church Family

If the church is the family of families, how are you to connect your own family to it? First, the church family and its leadership should never replace your responsibility for spiritual leadership. You cannot just send your children to the church to be taught the Word of God. The church programs should never replace your place as the primary leader of nurture and discipleship in your family.

Second, you need to make your family's involvement in the local church family a priority over involvement in other community or social activities or organizations. If it is not a priority to you, it will not be priority for them.

Third, we must participate in the financial needs of the extended church family just as we would in our own family. By so doing we teach our children to be generous and gracious to those in need.

Fourth, we must reinforce the outreach ministry of the local church family by seeing our family as an ideal platform for reaching out to neighboring families who do not know the grace of the gospel. Our homes are one of the best places where our neighbors can come and get to know us and through us hear the message of God's love and grace.

Part of managing your household well includes the connection you make with your local church family. If you are in ministry leadership, you need to work especially hard at this. Why? It is too easy for us to see our connection to the church as a job and inadvertently teach our children that the church is only the place their father works and not the place where the family connects with other families who love the Lord Jesus.

It is too easy for us to complain about the church in the hearing of our children. As they listen to us, they see the church through our complaints and learn to dislike and even hate the church because of what they hear from us.

As the leader in your family, what are you doing to connect your household with the household of God?

<u>Application Questions or Activities</u>

1. Do you have clear picture of the nature, composition, and purpose of the church. Take time to write a few sentences that describe these in your own words.

2. Have you neglected the church, either through not attending, or by not recognizing its importance in your time priorities?

3. Who in your church is hard to love? Write their names down. Pray for them. Reach out to them and actively seek reconciliation this week.

4. Where does your ministry threaten to take precedence over your family? What boundaries do you need to put in place to ensure this doesn't happen?

5. What activities and responsibilities outside your church compete with church?

6. How does your family demonstrate the love and glory of God to the community around it?

7. What are some practical ways you can support older members of your church family that have a difficult time caring for themselves?

Chapter 8: You and Your Government

Part of managing our household well includes our response to governing authorities.[51] Even though we may see ourselves as citizens of heaven, we still live in this world and are not exempt from the following authorities who have been given responsibility for community and national leadership. Romans 13:1-7 is very clear:

> *Let every person be subject to the governing authorities. For there is no authority except from God, and those that exist have been instituted by God. Therefore whoever resists the authorities resists what God has appointed, and those who resist will incur judgment. For rulers are not a terror to good conduct, but to bad. Would you have no fear of the one who is in authority? Then do what is good, and you will receive his approval, for he is God's servant for your good. But if you do wrong, be afraid, for he does not bear the sword in vain. For he is the servant of God, an avenger who carries out God's wrath on the wrongdoer. Therefore one must be in subjection, not only to avoid God's wrath but also for the sake of conscience. For because of this you also pay taxes, for the authorities are ministers of God, attending to this very thing. Pay to all what is owed to them: taxes to whom taxes are owed, revenue to whom revenue is owed, respect to whom respect is owed, honor to whom honor is owed.*

1 Peter 2:13-17 reinforces the call to submit to governing authorities:

> *Be subject for the Lord's sake to every human institution, whether it be to the emperor as supreme, or to governors as sent by him to punish those who do evil and to praise those who do good. For this is the will of God, that by doing good you should put to silence the ignorance of foolish people. Live as people who are free, not using your freedom as*

---

[51] Much of this chapter comes from Kroeker, Daryl, *Gripping the Essentials*, 130-134.

a cover-up for evil, but living as servants of God. Honor everyone. Love the brotherhood. Fear God. Honor the emperor.

The believer's relationship with Christ influences every relationship with authority. We are to submit and honor authority because it is God's will. We may not agree with, or like what those in authority say or command, but we are still to honor and obey (Titus 3:1-2).

Disobeying Civil Government

But is it ever right to disobey human government? There is agreement among Christians that there are times when a Christian should engage in civil disobedience.[52] There are stories in the Bible that help us understand possible exceptions. They include the Israelite midwives who disobeyed the orders of the Egyptian government that demanded they drown all the male babies born to the women of Israel (Exodus 1:15-21). The midwives disobeyed and allowed the baby boys to live by arriving at the birth late. God's response to their disobedience was that he dealt with them well (1:20).

The second example is found in Obadiah's refusal to obey the command of Queen Jezebel to kill the Lord's prophets (1 Kings 18:3-13). Jezebel had commanded that the prophets be killed, but Obadiah hid and fed one hundred of them in two caves. Although not stated directly, God's approval of Obadiah's action was implied through the subsequent deaths of the prophets of Baal (18:15-40).

The third example is found in the story of the Hebrew young men who refused to obey Nebuchadnezzar's command to worship his image of gold (Daniel 3). Shadrach, Meshach, and

---

[52] Norman L Geisler, *Christian Ethics: Contemporary Issues & Options* (Grand Rapids, Mich.: Baker Academic, 2010), 246.

Abednego refused to bow down and worship (3:12). Even though they were thrown into a fiery furnace for their lack of submission, God rescued them, and they were later honored by Nebuchadnezzar (3:23-30).

The fourth example is found in Acts 4:18-21. The religious authorities demanded that the apostles stop preaching and teaching in the name of Jesus, but they refused to stop. They told the authorities they were unable to stop speaking about what they had seen and heard, and they continued to preach and teach (4:31, 33). God vindicated their refusal to submit by answering their prayer for greater boldness (4:29).

In each of these cases, the authorities clearly asked the people involved to go against the direct commands of God. These exceptions tell us we are not obligated to obey human authorities when life and death are at stake, when we are commanded to worship something or someone other than the Lord God, and when we are commanded to stop preaching in the name of Jesus.

In his reflection on Psalm 58, which David wrote in response to wicked leadership, Steven Lawson says,

> Government leaders are appointed by God for the good of the people. They are to serve as his agents through whom he works to provide law and order for society (Rom. 13:1-6). But leaders often become corrupt, and they minister injustice to good people. What are God's people to do in such a situation? The Bible calls them to leave vengeance with the Lord…. They are to pursue peace with all men, submitting to those over them as much as possible. They must not take matters in their own hands. Ungodly leaders are an issue with which God must deal. But we can pray that the Lord will rebuke and remove such people.[53]

---

[53] Lawson and Anders, *Psalms 1-75*, 298.

Cautions Concerning Government

There are at least three cautions to consider in our relationship with governing authorities. First, never allow civil or political frustrations to distract you from the church's purpose and mission. The church exists to give glory to its Founder so that the world may get a glimpse of God's glory and love through it. We actively pursue this purpose, fighting to keep our focus on this mission and nothing else. Our goal is that all that we do in some way supports and perpetuates this mission. While many individual members can and should actively and peacefully participate in civil and political organizations and activities, we as a church will always actively pursue one thing and one thing alone: to bring glory to God in a way that our community around us can catch a glimpse of the glory of his character through us.

We should not use the pulpit as a political platform even if it were legal in our country. The church should not participate in protests (and no Christian should participate in violent protests) against a government we perceive as encroaching on our civil rights and freedoms. The only time Christians are given biblical permission to resist the government in any way, is (1) when preservation of helpless life deems it necessary, (2) when our freedom to worship Christ is threatened, (3) when our freedom to express our faith publicly – in a reasonable manner – is threatened, and (4), when obedience to the government would require direct disobedience to one or more biblical commands.

Our second caution is this: be very discerning when trying to decide if a particular decision or action by ruling authorities fits in one of these three categories. For example, when various national governments sought to stem the spread of Covid-19 by limiting the size of *all* public assemblies and eventually placing a temporary injunction against *any* public assembly, we would argue that this was not religious persecution. First, whether it was effective or not, it was an attempt to protect the public, not from religious ideologies, but from a physical threat that most perceived as very real and dangerous. Second, it in no way targeted religious assemblies. Sports, civil, and business assemblies were just as affected as the church. In many parts of our country the casinos were shut down for far longer than the church was. Third, the church was never denied its ability to worship, only to congregate. We were still free to have online services and for much of the time were allowed to congregate outside. Fourth, though for many it seemed way too long, it was indeed temporary.

In the West, many professed believers have confused an encroachment on their civil and political freedoms with religious persecution. Granted, these two forms of persecution often overlap. When the government actively moves to restrict all forms of participation in worship, as is the case in some parts of the world, it is clearly a case where both civil and religious rights are simultaneously being infringed upon. However, if you as a church leader are fighting side by side with the owner of a club dedicated to adult entertainment (something we understand happened recently in our home country of Canada), you can be pretty sure you are fighting on political or civil grounds, not religious grounds. The persecution you feel is not religious, and contrary to what many want to believe, the Bible does *not* give you permission to disobey or disrespect your government in these situations.

The third caution is not to over-react when we don't like the governing authorities or when we think that they are corrupt or incompetent. Both above-mentioned passages from Romans 13 and 1 Peter 2 were written while Israel was very uncomfortable with the oppressive, anti-Christian, very corrupt and often incompetent Roman authorities. Even under those conditions, Peter and Paul both demand that we respect and obey our government anyway. Even if we can't respect our ruler as a person, or their character and ideologies, we respect their position of authority over us.

Perhaps the biblical character who best demonstrates this is Daniel. We've already mentioned Shadrach, Meshach, and Abednego's refusal to bow down to Nebuchadnezzar's statue in Daniel 3 as an example of legitimate resistance to governmental authorities. A cursory glance at this story in Daniel 3 would reveal that they were as respectful and humble as they could be in their resistance. But it is Daniel himself who set the example for the way in which these young men would relate to their new governing authorities in the first chapter of Daniel.

Israel was invaded and conquered by Nebuchadnezzar, king of Babylon. He deported many of the leading people of Israel to Babylon and placed them in a government reeducation program. Daniel 1:3-4 states:

> *Then the king commanded Ashpenaz, his chief eunuch, to bring some of the people of Israel, both of the royal family and of the nobility, youths without blemish, of good appearance and skillful in all wisdom, endowed with knowledge, understanding learning, and competent to stand in the king's palace, and to teach them the literature and language of the Chaldeans.*

Daniel, Shadrach, Meshach, and Abednego were included among those conscripted into the university of Babylon. It is interesting to notice that Daniel and his friends never argued over what they are learning. Most certainly the "language and literature of the Chaldeans" would have been saturated with the religion and superstition of Babylonian culture,[54] and yet verse 5 tells us: *The king assigned them a daily portion of the food that the king ate, and of the wine that he drank. They were to be educated for three years, and at the end of that time they were to stand before the king.* Daniel and his colleagues were to do two things: go to school and change their diet. But it is not their education that causes them to chafe. They were willing to learn all that the king asked them to learn, because at this point, the king hasn't asked them yet to deny their faith or transfer their faith or allegiance to the Chaldean gods. So far, the ability to worship their God and express their own faith publicly in a reasonable manner have not been threatened.

Daniel does not resist authority until verse eight: *But Daniel resolved that he would not defile himself with the king's food, or with the wine that he drank. Therefore he asked the chief of the eunuchs to allow him not to defile himself.* To eat the king's food would have been in direct violation of God's commands concerning the dietary regulations found in the law given to Moses.

As Daniel and his friends face this challenge, they did not get angry, shout against the government, or arrange a protest. Instead, Daniel respectfully goes to his immediate authority and reasonably *asked the chief of the eunuchs to allow him not to defile himself.*

Not only was Daniel respectful and humble in his approach to his immediate authority, but he is also considerate of his concerns. The chief of the eunuchs is fearful that the king might notice that Daniel isn't as healthy as his peers because he hasn't been eating his assigned diet. He says it would *endanger my head with the king* (verse. 10). Daniel doesn't say anything close to "I don't care," or, "That's your problem." Rather, he asks the eunuch to allow him and his friends to eat a kosher diet for ten days and then determine

---

[54] See Bill T. Arnold and Bryan E. Beyer, *Readings from the Ancient Near East.* Grand Rapids, MI: Baker Academic, 2002.

whether their physical condition is better or worse than his peers (verses 12-13). Daniel agrees to submit to the steward's decision based on the results of this ten-day test. Clearly Daniel is as concerned for the Eunuch's head as he is his ability to follow his Lord's commands, so he leaves the decision up to God.

Daniel trusts that God will pave a way for him to be able to follow His commands. God does just that. Verse 9 says, *And God gave Daniel favor and compassion in the sight of the chief of the eunuchs…* Daniel would have never been able to present his concerns at all had God not already been at work in the relationship between Daniel and the chief of the eunuchs.

Most of us know the end of the story:

> *At the end of ten days it was seen that they were better in appearance and fatter in flesh than all the youths who ate the king's food. So the steward took away their food and the wine they were to drink, and gave them vegetables. As for these four youths, God gave them learning and skill in all literature and wisdom, and Daniel had understanding in all visions and dreams. At the end of the time, when the king had commanded that they should be brought in, the chief of the eunuchs brought them in before Nebuchadnezzar. And the king spoke with them, and among all of them none was found like Daniel, Hananiah, Mishael, and Azariah. Therefore they stood before the king. And in every matter of wisdom and understanding about which the king inquired of them, he found them ten times better than all the magicians and enchanters that were in all his kingdom* (Daniel 1:15-20).

Not only does God provide a path of obedience for Daniel and his peers, but God also blesses them beyond anything they could possibly imagine because they chose to obey Him, respectfully and humbly. This story is a graphic illustration of what Paul praises Christ for in Ephesians 3:20-21: *Now to him who is able to do far more abundantly than all that we ask or think, according to the power at work within us, to him be glory in the church and in Christ Jesus throughout all generations, forever and ever. Amen.*

To be sure, both Scripture and church history are replete with instances in which governmental resistance must be much more aggressive to accomplish the church's redemptive purposes. One need only look at the two occasions when Christ cleansed the Temple to see that authorities must at times be aggressively rebuked (Matt. 21:12-17; Mark 11:13-19; Lk 19:45-48; Jn. 2:13-16).[55] The fact that Jesus did this twice says he didn't give up when he at first didn't get his point across.[56]

But Jesus, Daniel, and others throughout history, including men like Dietrich Bonhoeffer, teach us not only *when* we should resist and disobey the government, but *how*.[57] It is important to neither overreact nor underreact. We ought to offer no more or no less resistance than is needed to accomplish the church's mission, and then do so with as much respect and humility as is possible.

Summary Principles

These are the summary principles and convictions that ought to guide our response to human government:

- God is sovereign over kings and nations (Daniel 2:21; Romans 13:1).

---

[55] Some might argue that wasn't against governmental but religious authorities, but Israel was a theocratic society. Church and state were so intimately connected that to resist one would be to resist the other.

[56] R.C. Sproul. *John: An Expositional Commentary,* St. Andrew's Expository Commentary Series, (Sanford FL: Reformed Trust Publishing, 2009) Olive Tree Ed.

[57] The dissidence of Dietrich Bonhoeffer against the Nazi party during World War II is perhaps the most famous example of legitimate governmental resistance in recent history. See Eric Metaxas, *Bonhoeffer: Pastor, Martyr, Prophet, Spy.* (Nashville, TN: Nelson Books, 2020).

- We are to obey those God has put in authority over us (Romans 13:1).

- We are to regularly pray for governing authorities (1 Timothy 2:1-4).

- We are to actively obey the commands of God, and this includes the work of making disciples of all nations (Matthew 28:18-20; Acts 4:13-20)

- We will need to choose to obey God rather than man when the demands of man go against the demands of God (Acts 5:29).

- God does not hold his people responsible to obey civil government when obedience would mean disobeying a direct command of God himself (Matthew 28:19-20 cf. Acts 4:18, 5:29).

- We need to be prepared to face the consequences of our disobedience (Daniel 3:17-18).

- We need to leave vengeance to the Lord and pray that God will rebuke and remove wicked leaders (Psalm 58).

- On occasions when our resistance to authorities is necessary, we do so as respectfully and humbly as we possibly can without compromising the truth.

Managing our household well includes our relationship with the authorities God puts over us and around us. If we are known as men who ignore, berate, and defy the authority of God in civil leadership, how can we expect those we lead in our family or in the church family to accept our place of authority?

Application Questions or Activities

1. Are there any areas in which you have confused an infringement of your civil and political freedoms as an attack on the church?

2. Are there any areas that your governing authorities are legitimately threatening helpless life or oppressing the church and its mission? Ask God what he may be calling you to do something about it.

3. Has your church lost sight of its mission? Where do you need to call your church back to its redemptive agenda?

4. Do you need to repent of your attitudes and feelings towards one or more governmental authorities? Be specific.

5. How often do you pray for your government? We challenge you to commit to praying at least once a week for your authorities by name. Ask the Lord to open their eyes that they may see and hear the grace and forgiveness offered to them in the gospel.

Chapter 9: You and Sound Doctrine

One of the main responsibilities of an elder or pastor is to know, teach and guard sound doctrine. Paul told the elders at Ephesus to

> *Pay careful attention to yourselves and to all the flock, in which the Holy Spirit has made you overseers, to care for the church of God, which he obtained with his own blood. I know that after my departure fierce wolves will come in among you, not sparing the flock; and from among your own selves will arise men speaking twisted things, to draw away the disciples after them. Therefore be alert* (Acts 20:28-30).

In Titus 1, Paul says an elder *must hold firm to the trustworthy word as taught, so that he may be able to give instruction in sound doctrine and also to rebuke those who contradict it* (Titus 1:9). To serve as an elder is to accept the responsibility of teaching and defending the gospel and the wonderful doctrines that surround it.

We need to admit that many men who find themselves in elder leadership think of themselves as part of a team that gives leadership to the church's programs. They see their responsibilities as the oversight of the facilities, finances, strategies and programs of the church. While this may be partly true, at the core of eldership is the responsibility to teach and guard sound doctrine. The buildings, budgets, policies, and programs are only the tools we use to teach and care for the people the Lord has entrusted to our care. They are not an end in and of themselves.

Learning Sound Doctrine

Teaching and guarding sound doctrine begins with the investment of significant time in learning sound doctrine. This goes far beyond our devotional reading. It takes more than listening and taking notes when we hear sermons. This learning demands careful intentional study of the doctrine that is central to the Christian faith.

Are you able to tell the story of the Bible from cover to cover? Do you understand how all the pieces come together to form one grand narrative of God's plan to glorify himself through the unfolding story of salvation? Are you able to show how Christ is central to whole story beginning from Genesis and working all the way through to the end of the book of Revelation?

Are you able to clearly explain the gospel? If someone asked you what it meant to be follower of Christ, could you tell them? Can you explain man's need for righteousness? Can you explain regeneration, conversion, justification, adoption, sanctification, preservation and glorification?

What do you know and understand about the character of God and his incommunicable and communicable attributes? Can you explain the Trinity of God? How about creation?

Are you able to articulate the doctrinal truths concerning the incarnation of Christ, his death and resurrection, and His work of atonement as the fulfillment of God's demands?

Are you able to explain the ministry of the Holy Spirit, including baptism, indwelling, sealing, filling, gifting, and production of fruit in the life of a believer?

Do you understand the essentials of the church including its nature, purpose, and membership? Can you clearly explain the meaning of baptism and the Lord's Supper? Do you understand the importance and process of church discipline? Can you describe qualifications and the role of elders and deacons? Do you know biblical answers to questions about the role of women in ministry leadership?

What do you know about the future as taught in the Bible? Can you outline the truths concerning the return of Christ, the tribulation, millennial reign, the judgments of believers and unbelievers and the eternal state?

These are some of the core doctrinal truths you need to learn before you consider entering the role of an elder. These are the truths you need to be able to teach to your household before you are given the responsibility of teaching them to the church family. These are the things you need to be articulate in so that you can defend and guard sound doctrine in your household and the church family.

Various Theological Approaches

If you want to go deeper in your study of biblical truth you need to understand that theology has been divided into five different categories. The better you understand doctrine from the perspective of each of these categories, the more wholistic your answer will be to the above-mentioned questions. As you go deeper in your study of the Bible and doctrine, it is important to have a sense of what these categories are and how they may shape the development of your theological thinking

1. Systematic Theology

This is the study of the major overarching doctrines of Scripture in their final form. Perhaps the most common form of theological study, systematic theology helps us understand what the whole Bible says about a particular doctrine. Some examples of said doctrines might be theology proper (the doctrine of God the Father), Christology (the doctrine of the person and work of Christ), pneumatology (the doctrine of the Spirit) soteriology (the doctrine of salvation, including the doctrines of election, justification and regeneration), ecclesiology (the doctrine of the Church), protology (study of creation) or eschatology (the study of end times).

2. Redemptive-Narrative Theology

This is commonly and perhaps misleadingly referred to as biblical theology or "whole-bible theology." Redemptive-Narrative Theology is the study of the Bible from the perspective that it is first and primarily the story of how God is saving us from us. Biblical theologians approach Scripture with the understanding that it is uniformly one grand story of redemption, made up of a myriad of smaller redemptive stories, teachings, prophecies, poems and wisdom literature all working together to develop and progress the grand narrative of redemption.

Redemptive-Narrative Theology is interested in how each doctrine develops throughout Scripture to grow into that final product. For example, we know that justification is from Christ alone, through faith alone, by grace alone. But Redemptive-Narrative Theology is interested in tracing the development of soteriology from its initial introduction in the "proto-euangelion"[58] in Genesis 3:15 through the Old Testament redemptive stories, covenants, sacrificial system, priesthood, prophecies, finally culminating in the climactic teachings of Jesus, and the rest of the New Testament authors. All this comes together to allow us to say with confidence: "Justification from Christ alone, through faith alone, by grace alone."

3. Exegetical Theology

This is the study of how to study Scripture. Exegetical Theology is interested in how we are to interpret and explain Scripture. It is not so interested in the doctrines themselves as it is in how we arrive at said doctrines. What is the process and

---

[58] The Latin term for "first evangelism."

methodology by which we interpret a given passage in the context of the whole of Scripture?

4. Historical Theology

This is the examination of how the church further refined our understanding of each doctrine. Historical Theology looks at how the early church arrived at our current canon of Scripture and how it dealt with various heresies and affirmed sound doctrine through church councils. It is interested in how the church grew, struggled, and was revived repeatedly, and how each time that cycle caused it to look afresh at the sacred doctrines of Scripture. It is interested in how the historical creeds, confessions and catechisms explain, defend, and refine sound doctrine and refute heresy. Historical Theology is interested in how the influential pastors and theologians of church history understood the sacred doctrines and how they explained them; how they further developed our understanding of said doctrine.

5. Practical Theology

This is the study of how we live out our doctrine. Practical Theology is interested in discovering the path between a passage's meaning to its original audience and what it means for us today. It is interested in what "lived out" doctrine looks like.[59]

While scholars and academics may have the luxury of concentrating on one category (perhaps even specializing further into subcategories within one of these main categories), it is necessary that a pastor be a bit more of a generalist. They must

---

[59] Some, including myself, would argue that this should not be considered a separate category of theology, but rather the climax and proper end to all theology. In the words of David Powlison, "All theology is practical. You have not completed your study of theology until it has effectively transformed and reshaped you and your functional worldview in some way." David Powlison from a lecture given in Biblical Counselling 101: *Dynamics of Biblical Change*, 2007.

have a fundamental grasp of each of these categories or their ministry and proclamation of the gospel will suffer in some way. Each of these theological categories complement each other and cooperate with each other to create a wholistic understanding of the gospel. As well, they keep each other in check. Exegetical theology, for example, doesn't allow us to come up with doctrine or application that isn't sufficiently supported by Scripture. Similarly, application done outside the context of systematics, or the redemptive narrative, may cause us to apply a particular passage of Scripture in a way that contradicts the whole of Scripture.

To be sure, we all have our inclinations, strengths and weaknesses. I (Richard) will never forget when Redemptive-Narrative Theology was first introduced to me in seminary. I felt like it breathed new life into what had become stale and lifeless exercises in cold academia for me. I became fascinated with Redemptive-Narrative Theology and spent much of my seminary years and afterward concentrating on the teachings of such biblical theologians as Herman Ridderbos, Geerhardus Vos, Meredith Kline, Graeme Goldsworthy, Tim Keller, D.A. Carson, and Craig Blomberg. Even now I gravitate toward the redemptive historical development of doctrine. But as pastors and elders we must have some fundamental and foundational understanding of each of the above five categories if we are to offer those under our care a wholistic understanding of the complete gospel message.

If there is one theological category that is yet more important than the others, it would have to be exegetical theology. There is a sense in which systematic theology, redemptive narrative theology, historical theology, and practical theology feeds us the proverbial fish. Exegetical Theology, sometimes referred to as exegesis, or hermeneutics teaches us how to catch the fish for ourselves. We will not here spend a great deal of time on exegetical methodology, opting instead to – hopefully – inspire and exhort you to spend a great deal of time in the future studying how to study Scripture. Propagation of much heresy and ignorance could be so easily avoided if we as pastors just understood and practiced basic principles of literary interpretation.

If this cursory glance at the scope and scale of theological understanding is intimidating, allow me to emphasize the necessity of theological education. We understand that there are areas in the world where your ability to pursue advanced education is seriously restricted, but if possible, the aspiring and current pastor/elder must academically prepare themselves for the ministry they are called to engage in. And even if finances or governmental restrictions do not allow you to pursue a Bible college or seminary degree, it may be possible to self-educate using online or printed material. Just be wise about whom you let teach you.

It is so important that we are properly trained and educated for the calling we are pursuing. We have heard many young men question this need of higher education, stating something along the lines of: "I just need my Bible and the Spirit," to which we often respond: "I am as afraid of an uneducated elder or pastor who would care for my soul as I would be of a heart surgeon trained in nothing more than basic first aid." We must know, and know well, the subject we aspire to teach or we will not be effective teachers. While good intentions and an effective teaching method is also necessary, there is no substitute for intimate knowledge of the subject matter.

If you are a graduate from a Bible college or seminary, do not allow your education to end at graduation. The pastor is called to be as much of a student of the Bible throughout his career as he is called to be a student in preparation for his career. Do not forsake well-balanced study of theology being taught by trusted teachers and pastors. For myself, I (Richard) dedicate at least five hours of my workweek in continuing education (in addition to studying for sermons, Bible studies, or counselling preparation). This continuing education may come in the form of books, professional journal articles, podcasts and blogs, professional conferences or lectures that are online or in class.

Guarding Doctrine in Your Teaching

Elders and pastors are not to be just students, but teachers. You need to be able to explain the core doctrines of the faith systematically and clearly in a way that is, at least to some degree, persuasive and convincing. You need to be able to share them informally in conversations with those in your household and you also need to be able to make a formal presentation of doctrinal truth when called upon. Paul told Timothy, *Do your best to present yourself to God as one approved, a worker who has no need to be ashamed, rightly handling the word of truth* (2 Timothy 2:15).

There is a difference between the gift of teaching and the skill of teaching. The gift of teaching is given by the Holy Spirit. The skill of teaching can be learned and developed, most often through practice. While the gift of teaching is certainly helpful, every elder is to be a teacher. They are to be able to make a Spirit-led presentation in a clear manner so that those who hear will not soon forget it but be impacted in their beliefs, their trust of God, and their resulting lifestyle.

At one point or another, you might find yourself in the pulpit or in front of a Bible class, charged as Timothy is charged by Paul in 2 Timothy 4:2 to *Preach the word; be ready in season and out of season; reprove, rebuke, and exhort with complete patience and teaching.* Your task will be to *rightly handle the word of truth* (2 Timothy 2:15). Even if you do not have the task of preaching and formal teaching, you at least should know what good preaching and teaching be able to encourage others to do it well.

To handle the word of truth well, all biblical teaching and preaching *must* be Christ-centered and redemptively focused. We cannot emphasize this enough. The Bible, from Genesis 1:1 to Revelation 22:21 is about Christ, with Christ and His redeeming work as its glorious climax. Biblical preaching and teaching must have as its primary goal the reorientation of our listeners' hearts and minds *from* all distraction *to* their desperate need of Christ and his complete sufficiency and willingness to fulfill that need. The first question of the Heidelberg Catechism asks, "What is your only comfort in life and in death?" The following answer is given:

> That I am not my own, but belong with body and soul, both in life and in death, to my faithful Saviour Jesus Christ. He has fully paid for all my sins with his precious blood, and has set me free from all the power of the devil. He also preserves me in such a way that without the will of my heavenly Father not a hair can fall from my head; indeed, all things must work together for my salvation. Therefore, by his Holy Spirit he also assures me of eternal life and makes me heartily willing and ready from now on to live for him.[60]

The primary focus of our teaching and preaching *must* remind our listeners of these truths every time we stand in front of them.

We are to preach and teach obedience, but only in the context of worship and gratitude for Christ's perfect and complete obedience on our behalf even unto the cross. We are to inform

---

[60] The Heidelberg Catechism. Open Domain. http://www.heidelberg-catechism.com/en/lords-days/1.html

our listeners of sound doctrine, but only insofar as it helps them fall ever more deeply in love with their Saviour. We are called at times to rebuke and admonish, but only for the purpose of calling wayward sheep home to their only comfort in life and in death. We are even called to warn our listeners of the eternal consequences of unbelief and unrepentance, but we do so not to inspire fear, but to give them a glimpse of God's justice and holiness. And any preaching on hell should always be backed up with an invitation to receive Christ's forgiveness and grace through repentance. In the words of Dwight L. Moody, "No one should ever preach on the topic of hell without a tear in his eye."[61]

Also, to handle the word of truth well, we strongly encourage you as an elder or pastor to make a commitment to expository preaching and teaching. Expository sermons focus almost exclusively on one passage of Scripture and extract both the central theme and the main points of the sermon from that specific passage. As the preacher or teacher walks through the passage verse by verse, or paragraph by paragraph, the main points of the passage become the main points of the preaching or teaching. One of the best ways to do expository preaching is to work through a book of the Bible from beginning to end.

This kind of preaching requires a great deal of exegetical research along with humility and prayer to discern what the human author, led by the Spirit, was trying to say to the original audience. Wise and compassionate exposition takes the congregation on a journey *from* what the text meant to the original audience *to* what it means to today's audience, all the while remaining faithful to the intensions of the Spirit-led original author.

Expository sermons are less prone to what exegetical

------

[61] Dwight L. Moody. AZQuotes, https://www.azquotes.com/quote/1395348

theologians call "eisegesis" than topical[62] or thematic[63] sermons. Eisegesis is when the interpreter reads his own opinions and presuppositions into a text rather than allowing the text to dictate the message and exercise authority over the interpretative process. If we approach the text with our own agenda, it is so easy to see that text as teaching that which we want it to say, whether it does or not. This is not to say that there is *never* a time for a topical or a thematic sermon, but it is important to use these methods sparingly. When the occasion calls for a topical or thematic sermon, take extra precaution to remain faithful to Scripture and sound doctrine.

To rightly handle the word of truth, it is also important to ensure your mouth and life are preaching the same gospel. Correct theology presented well isn't helpful to your audience unless they see that your actions and attitudes demonstrate that which you are asking them to believe and trust in.

Good expositional teaching guards against false teaching and heresy. When the truth is clearly affirmed and articulated by the elders, it will guard against the church family being distracted and disrupted by personal opinions and incorrect ideas.

John MacArthur puts it so well when he says,

> In Paul's list of criteria for excellent servant leaders, he exhorts his apprentice, Timothy, to be a serious student of Scripture. First Timothy 4:6 speaks of being "constantly nourished on the words of the faith and of the sound doctrine which you have been following." Paul knew that

---

[62] A topical sermon is a sermon that picks a topic (for example: worship, good works, or salvation), and bounces around the bible to pick different passages to support different points of the message.

[63] Like expository sermons, a thematic sermon will often camp out in one text, but contrary to exposition, in a thematic sermon a preacher will pick a theme, then find a text that teaches on that theme (remember, exposition extracts both the theme and the main points from the passage).

Timothy was already well-versed in the truth. "From childhood you have known the sacred writings which are able to give you the wisdom that leads to salvation through faith which is in Christ Jesus" (2 Timothy 3:15). This is an exhortation to stay immersed in Scripture and faithful to its truth.

Being "constantly nourished" connotes a continual process of self-feeding on the Word of God. The godly pastor needs to hunger for the truth the way a starving baby cries out for milk (1 Peter 2:2). Timothy's biblical intake was critical if he was going to "be diligent to present [himself] approved to God as a workman who does not need to be ashamed, accurately handling the word of truth" (2 Timothy 2:15). At the same time, Paul charged him to "avoid worldly and empty chatter, for it will lead to further ungodliness, and their talk will spread like gangrene. Among them are Hymenaeus and Philetus, men who have gone astray from the truth" (2 Timothy 2:16-18).

God's servants are mandated to heed Paul's warning. Despite that clear command, many expose their biblical illiteracy every time they step into the pulpit. Others are more interested in and enamored of their own insights and opinions, rather than accurately and fully proclaiming what God has revealed in Scripture. The result is always a weak, shallow congregation that proliferates untrained and unqualified leaders who extend their pastor's ignorance exponentially. Today the church is overrun with "leaders" who have human skills, but no passion for biblical scholarship.

Hand in hand with the consistent study of God's Word is the ability to avoid the things that most often distract from that study. God's people need to be fed out of the overflow of the pastor's deep study of Scripture—not some scraps he was able to pull together at the last minute. Such weakness in the pulpit leads to weakness throughout the church. Good communication skills may entertain, but they are useless if the pastor is not unleashing God's Word.[64]

Managing your household well includes your management of sound doctrine. You must hold a high view of Scripture and its foundational place in your ministry to your household and the household of God (2 Timothy 3:16-17). With Timothy, you must,

> *preach the word; be ready in season and out of season; reprove, rebuke, and exhort with complete patience and teaching. For the time is coming when people will not endure sound teaching, but having itching ears they will accumulate for themselves teachers to suit their own passions, and will turn away from listening to the truth and wander off into myths. As for you, always be sober-minded, endure suffering, do the work of an evangelist, fulfill your ministry* (2 Timothy 4:2-5).

Stay calm and watchful. Don't run from trouble. Keep the gospel in the center of your teaching. Complete what God has given you to do.

Question Your Calling

As you consider what it means to know, teach, and guard sound doctrine you need to question your calling. *Not many of you should become teachers, my brothers, for you know that we who teach will be judged with greater strictness* (James 3:1). This should scare some of us. Remember that there is only one competency-based qualification of an elder or a pastor. They must be *able to teach* (1

---

[64] John MacArthur, "The Servant Leader Studies," Grace to You, cty.org/blog, May 27, 2022. Accessed May 31, 2022.

Tim. 3:2). All other qualifications refer to character. It is our character that is the basis on which *we will be judged with greater strictness.* If an elder or pastor must be *able to teach,* and James says that not many of you *should become teachers,* then the logical conclusion is that not many should aspire to eldership. A cursory glance at both early and modern church history will reveal a myriad of examples of unqualified ministry leaders both from the perspective of their character and their competency. Don't be one of them. Honestly evaluate your doctrine, character, and competency before answering what you perceive as a call to church leadership. No matter what you may feel, or what others in the church family may think, no one is truly called to be an elder or pastor if they do not have the character and competency of an elder. If you are not willing or able to put in the hard work to learn doctrine, the competency to teach it, or the courage to defend it, you should not be an elder.

If you find after honest evaluation, that you do not have what it takes to be an elder, do not devalue yourself. Paul argues persuasively in 1 Corinthians 12 that we all have different but equally important roles in the body of Christ.[65] We all are united under one leader, that is Christ. We have a common bond of all being part of one body. And we have one mission: the glorification of Christ and the edification of each other. But though we are unified in leadership, bonding, and mission, we are diverse in our giftings and the roles we play in accomplishing this. No one is more or less important than another. We are all used by God, in various and sundry ways, to accomplish His redemptive plan in the church, your community and the world.

Remember as well that all work done to the glory of God is

---

[65] In chapter 11 you will find *A Word About Deacons.* As you read it you may discover you are better gifted to serve as a deacon rather than an elder.

sacred. Whether you are called by God to be a plumber, truck driver, doctor, teacher or vegetable farmer, your calling is no more or no less noble, dignified, respectable or important to the kingdom than that of an elder, pastor, or missionary. So, *whatever you do, in word or deed, do everything in the name of the Lord Jesus, giving thanks to God the Father through him* (Colossians 3:17).

Application Questions and Activities

1. How would you measure your theological maturity? Use the chart below for your evaluation.

A Mature Faith

a. One who is not a new Christian.

> *... he must not be a recent convert*
>
> *... or he may become conceited and fall under the same judgment as the devil* (1 Tim. 3:6)

Weak				**Strong**
1	2	3	4	5

b. One who has a solid grounding and understanding of the Word.

> *... he must hold firmly to the trustworthy message as it has been taught*
>
> *... so that he can encourage others by sound doctrine and refute those who oppose it* (Titus 1:9)

Weak				**Strong**
1	2	3	4	5

c. One who is able to lead others into spiritual growth.

> *... able to teach* (1 Tim. 3:2)
>
> *... so that he can encourage others by sound doctrine and refute those who oppose it* (Titus 1:9)

Weak				**Strong**
1	2	3	4	5

d. One who lives as an example to others.

> *... being examples to the flock* (1 Peter 5:3)

Weak				**Strong**
1	2	3	4	5

A Teachable Mind

a. One who is balanced.

> ... *temperate* (1 Tim. 3:2)
>
> ... *disciplined* (Titus 1:8)
>
> An elder's judgment must never be clouded by extremes. He must have a clear perspective on life and be stable, steadfast, clear and biblical in his thinking.

Weak				**Strong**
1	2	3	4	5

b. One who is willing to learn and able to teach.

> ... *able to teach* (1 Tim. 3:2)
>
> An elder must be able to learn, teach, and guard sound doctrine as well as be willing to accept correction when errors are pointed out.

Weak				**Strong**
1	2	3	4	5

c. One who is fair.

> ... *upright* (Titus 1:8)
>
> An elder must be willing to be just and fair in all his dealings. He must seek to make decisions based on biblical principles and not personalities.

Weak				**Strong**
1	2	3	4	5

2. As you review the qualities outlined above how do you measure up? Has weakness in any of these areas disqualified you from leadership at this time? Where do you need to keep growing? What do you need to do to progress toward godliness in these areas? What are you going to do?

3. Do you love the word of God? Does spending time studying your Bible, beyond devotional times, have a high priority in your schedule? What might you need to do to adjust your schedule to make significant time for learning sound doctrine?

4. Are you able to give someone an overview of the grand narrative of the Bible? Can you describe and defend the essential doctrinal truths? What would help you be able to do this?

5. Are you prepared to teach the Bible? What has been your experience in teaching or preaching? What do you like about it or what do you fear? What do you need to learn or do to improve your ability to teach or preach confidently and clearly?

6. Have you questioned your calling to be an elder or pastor? Are you able and willing to learn, teach and guard sound doctrine?

7. Is there something else you would rather do than be an elder? Is there another place of ministry you would prefer or are better gifted or suited for within the church family?

Chapter 10: A Word About Women as Elders

This can be a controversial subject loaded with emotion and passion on both sides of the issue. There are those who are very restrictive in their understanding of the role of women in the ministry of the church, and there are those on the other side who see no restrictions on the ministry activities and leadership that women can be involved in. As you read this chapter, please be patient as we walk through various biblical texts in an attempt to understand what God desires.

As we wrestle with the question of whether women can serve as elders, we need to be aware of the dangers we can encounter. The first danger is letting culture overrule the Bible. As Philip Ryken says, allowing the "tail of culture to wag the dog of biblical truth.[66] In the minds of many contemporary people, excluding women from church eldership is seen as sexist, discriminatory and one more example of male dominance.[67]

There is also the danger of allowing our reaction to church history or church tradition dictate how Scripture should be applied. For example, there has been a despicable disdain for women that has been displayed by men throughout church history. But we cannot overreact to the church's sin by ignoring the true biblical teaching that might have been used historically to wrongly justify its actions.

The third danger is to allow our opinion, or another person's opinion distort our understanding of the Scripture. This includes allowing a family member's or friend's ministry leadership and activities to determine the meaning of a particular passage.

Fourth, there is the resistance of our own sin nature which

---

[66] Ryken, *1 Timothy*, Reformed Expository Commentary, 87.
[67] Strauch, Biblical Eldership, 51.

detests submission to what God says because it wants us to be in control of our lives and belief systems.

The Core Question

Here is the core question: What is the role of women in the leadership of the church? In the simplest of terms, God has commanded men, husbands, fathers to lead their families in discipleship, worship, and service. God then asks the best family leaders to lead his family, the church. This means that only qualified men are to serve in the overseeing elder and pastor role in the church. Every ministry is available to men and women based on their giftedness, except the role of elder or pastor leadership. We need to be careful here because the question is not about women in ministry. Women are needed and called to be in ministry. The question is about women in the elder pastor role of the local church.

The Biblical Evidence

There are four main pieces of biblical evidence to support that men and women have complementary roles in both the family and the church family – where men are called to lead, and women are called to follow their leadership. The first piece of evidence is found in the nature of the Trinity of God. The members of the Trinity are equal in power and possess equally all the attributes of God. However, God the Father has ultimate authority over the events in history (Acts 1:7; Mark 13:32; 1 Corinthians 15:24; Daniel 2:20-21). The members of the Trinity are equal in every way but they have different roles or functions. Consider the work of creation: God the Father spoke the creative words to bring the universe into existence; the Son carried out these creative decrees (John 1:3; Colossians 1:16); the Holy Spirit was active in moving over the face of the waters, manifesting God's immediate presence in his creation (Genesis 1:2). Consider also the work of redemption: God the Father planned redemption and sent his Son into the world (John 3:16; Galatians 4:4; Ephesians 1:9-10); the Son obeyed the Father and accomplished redemption for us (John 6:38; Hebrews 10:5-7); the Holy Spirit was sent by the Father and the Son to apply and complete the work of redemption that was planned by the Father and begun by the Son (John 3:5-8; 14:26; 15:26; 16:7; Romans 8:13; Ephesians 1:13-14; 1 Peter 1:2; Acts 1:8). Since men and women are created in the image of God, the difference in roles is a picture or reflection of the image of God.

The second piece of evidence is found in the creation order. In the two most important passages on the topic, 1 Corinthians 11:3-16 and 1 Timothy 2:11-15, the reason Paul gives for gender distinction is found in the creation of Adam and Eve. In 1 Timothy, Paul appeals to the order of creation (2:13) and the order of deception (2:14). In 1 Corinthians 11, Paul points out that the woman was made from man and for man (11:8-9). In Genesis 1:26, God says, *Let us make man in our image, according to our likeness.* Then in verse 27 we read, *So God created man in his own image; he created him in the image of God; he created them male and female.* Then God sends them out with a joint task, *God blessed them, and God said to them, "Be fruitful, multiply, fill the earth, and subdue it. Rule the fish of the sea, the birds of the sky, and every creature that crawls on the earth"* (1:28). Men and women are created equal. Together they share God's image and are given the same task to be fruitful, and to subdue and rule the earth.

In the completion of the task assigned by God, men and women are given different roles. Adam was created first (Genesis 2:7; 18-23). This is significant because throughout the Old Testament the firstborn in a family is seen as the leader in that family for that generation.[68] In 1 Timothy 2:13, Paul uses the fact that Adam was created first as his reason for restricting women from the elder role in the church.

It also needs to be noted that Eve was created as a help for Adam (Genesis 2:18). The helper occupies a subordinate position to the one being helped. This should not be taken to mean that a woman is less important than a man, but simply that there is a difference in roles. It was also Adam who gave Eve her name (Genesis 2:23). He had previously named the animals (Genesis 2:19-20, indicating he had authority over them. In his naming of the woman, he indicates he has a leadership responsibility over her as well. It is also interesting that God named humanity "man" and not "woman" (Genesis 5:2), suggesting the leadership role belonged to the man.

The third piece of evidence which supports the position that men and women have complementary roles in both the family and the church family comes from 1 Corinthians. In 1 Corinthians 11:2-16 and 14:33-35, Paul applies this understanding of male and female to corporate worship. Paul begins his argument in 11:3 by stating his main idea: *Christ is the head of every man, and the man is the head of the woman, and God is the head of Christ.* Again, we see equality and complementary roles. Paul says male-female roles operate in a similar way as the roles in the Trinity. While the Father and Son are equally God eternally, they have unique roles: the Son subjects himself to the Father. In the same way, a husband and wife are equal, and yet the husband is called to lead and have authority, while his wife is called to help and honor her husband.

In 1 Corinthians 11:4-7, Paul applies this to the specific issue of how men and women dress for corporate worship. In his

---

[68] Wayne A Grudem, *Systematic Theology: An Introduction to Biblical Doctrine (2nd Edition)*, Second Edition., 2020, 587.

culture, a woman wore a head covering as a symbol of her marital status. Paul urges them to dress in a manner that reflected their roles as women, citing the created order in Genesis 2 as his reason for maintaining the distinction (11:8-9). He is saying that gender roles were a part of God's good creation, and the woman needs to recognize her role and dress and act accordingly. This does not mean she is in any way inferior to man, but that each are created complementary to each other. Both men and women need to be faithful to the roles God gave them.

When Paul mentions the silence of women in 1 Corinthians 14, the greater context is still public worship, but now he is addressing specifically the giving and weighing of prophecies (14:29-33). The nature of New Testament prophecy demanded that the appropriate leaders discern what was from the Lord and what might not be from him (14:29). Not every prophecy is truly a word from the Lord. It is in this context that Paul argues that *women should be silent in the churches* (14:34). It is obvious that Paul does not impose absolute silence, as earlier in this same letter he allows women to pray and prophecy in church, if she does so in a non-subversive manner, as is fitting with her role (11:5). So it is not the praying and prophesying which is forbidden, but it is in the context of weighing or judging prophecies that women need to be silent and learn. This weighing or judging is part of the elder role (See Acts 20:28-31).

The fourth piece which supports the position that men and women have complementary roles in both the family and the church family comes from 1 Timothy 2:8-15. When speaking about the public worship gatherings of the church, Paul urges the men to lift their hands in prayer instead of in quarrelling, and the women to dress modestly and to strive to live in a way appropriate for godly women. In verse 11, Paul urges that women should learn, even though this was largely counter-cultural at the time. But like all good students, they should learn in a submissive, quiet way. He then states in verse 12, *I do not allow a woman to teach or to have authority over a man; instead, she is to remain quiet.*

It must be noted that in 1 Timothy 2, Paul is not simply addressing a unique situation in the church at Ephesus that is no longer relevant today. In verse 8 Paul indicates that the instructions he is giving about public worship are *in every place*. This phrase can be understood as being the same as the phrase *all the churches* that is use by Paul in other passages (Romans 16:4, 16; 1 Cor. 7:17; 2 Cor. 8:18; 11:28). The directions in 1 Timothy 2 were not just for the Ephesian church family. These instructions were for every place and every church. Therefore, Paul was not addressing a unique Ephesian problem, or a cultural issue found in that context.

As he writes under the inspiration of the Holy Spirit, Paul points to two specific activities that are outside the roles of women and are therefore not permitted in the church family: teaching Christian doctrine to men and exercising authority directly over men in the church.

Paul is not trying to decertify women as teachers or leaders. Nor is he giving all men a license to instruct and rule. Men had to meet the strict requirements of 1 Timothy 3 and Titus 1. Paul's instructions are not about superiority or inferiority of persons or gender. Rather, he is seeking to promote regular worship order. While men and women could prophecy and pray (1 Cor. 11:4-5), there came a time in the assembly when the elders instructed and exhorted and taught sound doctrine.

Paul then gives two reasons for maintaining gender role distinction (1 Timothy 2:13-14). Both these reasons are from Genesis 2 and 3. The first is the created order, simply meaning that Adam came before Eve. Paul does not allow women to teach Christian doctrine to men and exercise authority directly over men in the church, because of God's created order. To abandon gender distinction is to act in contradiction to the way God created and designed mankind as male and female. Adam was formed first, and therefore has responsibility for Eve. This is not cultural or unique to Ephesus or the first century but is a universal principle to be applied to all times and cultures, because this is how God designed male and female relationships to work.

Paul's second reason for gender role distinction is in 1 Timothy 2:14 and also comes from Genesis 3. Paul writes, *And Adam was not deceived, but the woman was deceived and transgressed.* Some have argued that Paul is stating that women should not teach or have authority since they are more easily deceived than men. However, Paul does not make this connection. Paul is simply comparing Eve's deception to the situation in Ephesus. Like Eve, the women in Ephesus were being tempted to reject their role and usurp male authority. They needed to learn from Eve's mistake and not fall into the same situation.

It is interesting to notice at this point that the text says *Adam was not deceived.* This means that as Adam stood beside Eve at the forbidden tree, he knew what he was doing. Satan blinded Eve, but Adam had his eyes wide open. Adam followed Eve when he should have led her. Adam followed Eve when he should have resisted the serpent's advance. As a result, Adam was held accountable because it was his task to lead his family into spiritual health. Adam is held responsible for sin (Genesis 3:9; Romans 5:12). The woman is condemned because she was deceived, and the man was condemned because he knowingly failed to exercise the leadership task God gave him. Both men and women are condemned, and their condemnation is linked specifically to their roles related to their gender. Rather than submitting to the man, the woman submitted to the serpent. Rather than exercise his right and responsibility as the family leader, Adam gave that task to Eve.

1 Timothy 2:15 is a difficult verse. In it Paul pictures one of the unique roles of women: childbearing. He says, *But she will be saved through childbearing, if they continue in faith, love, and holiness, with good sense.* Just as one unique aspect of the role of men centers around teaching and exercising authority, one unique aspect of the role of women is childbearing. This is not saying that childbearing is the only task women are called to – just as teaching and exercising authority are not the only tasks men are called to – but it is a significant distinctive role that women are uniquely designed to fulfill. This is the role that God gave to women and not to men. But what does it mean when it says *she will be saved through childbearing?* Does it mean the woman is saved or redeemed because she has children? It cannot mean that because salvation is by grace through faith in the Lord Jesus Christ and not of works. Does it mean she is better woman because she has children? It cannot mean that either because throughout history there have been millions of women who have never had children but are loved and cared for by our Heavenly Father the same as those who have borne children.

To find an answer we must notice the words in the last half of the verse: *if they continue in faith and love and holiness, with self-control.* The reality or evidence of anyone's salvation is seen when they persevere or continue in *faith, love, and holiness, with self-control* while carrying out whatever the Lord's calling is in their lives. What Paul tells women is that one of the unique callings or roles they have from the Lord is childbearing. As they fulfill that call and role, or any other task God has given them, they are not to seek after the role and responsibilities given to men in leading their family and the church family.

The Local Church Context

How do Paul's instructions work out in a church context? What role does Paul have in mind when he prohibits women from teaching and exercising authority? A survey of the Pastoral Epistles reveals that Paul is referring to the two most prominent tasks of the ἐπισκοπή (elder/overseer).[69] Paul is prohibiting women from fulfilling the governing and teaching role of overseer. This indicates that godly men are called to be pastors and elders and to fulfill church governance roles. Everything else is open for participation and leadership by both men and women

This is not about superiority. Women can out-think, out-talk, are more relationally in tune than men. They are naturally empathetic, more intuitive about where people are and are generally better at communication.

This is also not about suitability for leadership. It is a statistical fact that women read more Christian books than men and attend church gatherings in far greater numbers. The elder and pastoral role is not about who can lead the best. Instead, it must be about the Bible's instructions on church leadership as prescribed by the Holy Spirit.

While the role of elder is preserved for men who lead their families well (1 Timothy 3:1-7), women fulfilled many significant roles in the New Testament church. Phoebe served as a deacon in the church at Cenchrae (Romans 16:1-2). Junia served alongside her husband Andronicus (Romans 16:7). Paul says Eudia and Syntyche served and *contended for the gospel at my side* (Philippians 4:3). Lydia of Philippi was a wealthy merchant who appears to

---

[69] See 1 Tim 3:2; 4:11-16; 5:17; 6:2; 2 Tim 2:2; 24-25; Titus 1:9.

have led her household to Christ, hosted a home church and financed Paul's ministry (Acts 16:11-15, 40). Women have been gifted by the Holy Spirit for ministry in the church family and are free to use their gifts and abilities outside of the role of an elder. Only qualified men are to serve in the elder overseeing role in which they are responsible for the spiritual leadership, teaching, and care of the church family.

<u>Application Questions or Activities</u>

1. Why are men called to lead their families? Why does God call specially qualified men to lead his family? Are you committed to obey what the Bible teaches on this topic?

2. How can we encourage women to think biblically on this subject of serving without feeling rejected or inferior?

3. What are some of the ways and places women can be involved in ministry leadership without being an elder?

Chapter 11: What About Deacons?

The focus of our study is on the character qualities required of one who desires to be an elder or pastor. However, there is another leadership title that is used of ministry leaders who serve the church family. This is the title of Deacon.

What is a Deacon?

The term *deacon,* as used in the New Testament, does not always refer to the official leadership office or position of deacon. It is most often used as term for serving or ministering. A study of its non-formal use gives great insight into the richness of deacon service. It is used as:

- Waiters at tables (Luke 17:8; Acts 6:2, John 2:5,9; Luke 10:40; Matt. 8:15; Matt. 4:11)
- Rendering service to another (Matt. 22:1-14; John 12:26; Matt. 20:26-28; Mark 10:45; 1 Cor. 16:15; Heb. 1:14).
- A monetary ministry (Luke 8:3; 2 Cor. 8-9).
- Governmental official (Rom. 13:4).
- Christ as servant (Rom. 15:8; Mark 10:45; Matt. 20:26; John 13:1-17; John 12:26).

The basic concept underlying the word "deacon" is that of voluntary, love-prompted service for the benefit of others. It is a service that desires the true welfare of those ministered to.

Deacons are the servants of the church. In one sense we are all deacons and servants of the church, but it appears that the office of deacon is a recognized position that is responsible for particular kinds of service. Deacons typically look after ministry details, including the distribution of care, leadership of ministry programs, and oversight of finances (Acts 6:1-6; Romans 16:1-2).

But before we see them as a lesser leader than the elder, we need to remember the words of Jesus. He said to his disciples who were arguing with each other, *The greatest among you will be your servant. Whoever exalts himself will be humbled, and whoever humbles himself will be exalted* (Matthew 23:11-12), and *If anyone wants to be first, he must be last and servant of all* (Mark 9:35) and *whoever is greatest among you should become like the youngest, and whoever leads, like the one serving* (Luke 22:26). Of himself, Jesus said, *For even the Son of Man did not come to be served, but to serve, and to give his life as a ransom for many* (Mark 10:45; Matthew 20:28). By his example and his words, Jesus elevated service to a place of honor and so we ought to consider the deacons of the church as people of honor.

The office of *Deacon* as described in the New Testament (Acts 6:1-7; Phil. 1:1; 1 Tim. 3:8-12) reveals the following facts about Deacons:

1. Deacons are closely related to elders and serve under the direction and supervision of them.
2. The word *deacon* is always plural. The office of deacon consists of a corporate body or team of servants.
3. Deacons must meet specific qualifications that are similar to those required of elders.

The New Testament lists no fixed duties for deacons. As their name indicates, deacons are good servants who serve in whatever capacity needed. They adjust their ministry to meet the needs at hand. There is great latitude in the type of work they do.

Who Qualifies to be a Deacon?

The qualifications of deacons as listed in the New Testament (Acts 6:3; 1 Tim. 3:8-12) include the following:

1. **A Good Reputation**
   a) One who is respected (1 Tim 3:8). The word *respected* means to be orderly or well arranged. A deacon is not to

be the kind of person that runs from crisis to crisis because he is disorganized, but his life must be marked by consistency and order.

b) One who is *known to be full of the Spirit and wisdom* (Acts 6:3). They are to be known by their relationship with the Lord.

c) One who is blameless (1 Tim. 3:9-10. The word *blameless* does not mean perfect. But the characteristic pattern of life must be in line with biblical standards. There must not be any verifiable, unresolved charges of wrongdoing that could be brought against him.

d) One who displays godliness in financial dealings (1 Tim. 3:8). A deacon is not to join the ministry team for the sake of material advantage. They are to be a person of complete integrity in financial dealings.

2. Exercises Self-Control

a) One who is not controlled by artificial stimulants (1 Tim. 3:8). A deacon is not to be attached or addicted to artificial stimulants that would replace the control of the Holy Spirit. They are to be in control of their passions and appetites (Gal. 5:16-26).

b) One who is sincere (1 Tim. 3:8). Their word must be trustworthy. They cannot say one thing to one person and another to another. Yes must mean yes and no means no. They cannot say one thing and do another. They must be a person of their word.

3. Healthy Relationships

a) One who is faithful (1 Tim. 3:12). They must be a one-woman kind of a man or a one-man kind of a woman.

They must be a devoted covenant keeper. They must not be flirtatious in any relationship with the opposite gender.

b) One who displays godly leadership at home (1 Tim. 3:12). They must be a servant of those in their household. They must be one who has a positive influence in their home. They must be one who manages all their responsibilities well, including time, money, possessions, and relationships.

c) One whose spouse is living a godly life (1 Tim. 3:11). As a husband, he must have an impact on his wife. She must be the kind of person who loves and lives for the Lord so as not to hinder the work God has called him to.

4. A Mature Faith

a) One whose maturity has been observed over time (Acts 6:3 and 1 Tim. 3:10). A deacon must have an observable faith. They must be proven over time. The word *tested* means to be examined using pressure to see how they perform.

b) One whose life is built on solid biblical foundations (1 Tim. 3:9). A deacon must be a person of the Word, who is known to diligently study and obey it. They need to know the Word and demonstrate godliness in everyday life.

The qualifications of a deacon are almost identical to those of an elder (1 Timothy 3:8-13). The main exception is that they are not required to be able to teach sound doctrine, since teaching and guarding doctrine is the role of an elder.

Just because the deacon isn't required to *teach* doctrine, doesn't mean they don't have to *know* doctrine. There is a certain maturity required of those who serve as deacons. That maturity is not only built on the humility that a deacon must cultivate but it must also come from an ever-growing intimacy with the Lord. The foundation of their relationship with God is an ever-increasing knowledge of who he is, what he has done, what he is now doing and what he has promised to do. They also need a deep awareness that God will do everything he has said as he fulfills his promises. In other words, deacons too must know doctrine.

What Does a Deacon Do?

In Acts 6 we read of the appointment of the first deacons. A specific need was brought to the attention of the apostles: There were widows who were being left out of the daily distribution of the food. Instead of getting involved in the day-to-day ministry of the growing fellowship, the apostles set their priorities as prayer and the teaching of the Word of God. However, to alleviate the problem they asked that deacons be chosen who would take it upon themselves to alleviate the problem and meet the needs of these widows. Their task was very specific and focused.

While the New Testament lists no fixed duties for deacons, their name indicates they are good servants who serve in whatever capacity is needed. They adjust their ministry under the direction of the elders to meet the needs at hand. As a result, there is great latitude in the specific type of work they may be asked to do. But never are they required to do fill the leadership role required of an elder.

Can Women Serve as Deacons?

In 1 Timothy 3:11 it says, *Their wives likewise must be dignified, not slanderous, but soberminded, faithful in all things.* Some Bible translations translate the Greek word gynē as *wives* (ESV & CSB). Some translate the word as *women* (NASB, NIV) In translating it *women*, some suggest this is talking about female deacons, also known as deaconesses.[70] Philip Ryken writes:

> The strongest reason for thinking that these women were deaconesses is the way they are introduced. Both verse 8 and verse 11 contain the word "likewise" (*hōsautōs*), which sounds as if it introduces a new office. Furthermore, these women are to be "dignified" (1 Tim. 3:11), which is the same phrase used to describe deacons (1 Tim. 3:8). Both these verses are grammatically dependent on the main verve in verse 2, which strengthens the connection between them. Taken together, these parallels make it sound as if the women Paul had in mind were to fulfill a separate but equal office in the church.[71]

However, Ryken goes on to give four reasons why *wives* is a better translation.[72]

1. If Paul meant deaconesses, he would have said so.
2. The word "woman" is such a common term that it probably would not have been designated as an office in the church.
3. The word *gynaikas* is also found in 1 Timothy 3:12 where it clearly refers to the wife of a deacon. Paul has the same women in view in both verses.
4. One short verse of instructions embedded into the qualifications for deacons is too brief and inadequate to give detailed qualifications for deaconesses.

While there is evidence of women serving as deacons (Phoebe in Romans 16:1), some suggest we can't go there too quickly from

---

[70] Donald Guthrie, ed., *The New Bible Commentary: Revised* (Grand Rapids, Mich: Eerdmans, 1973), 1173.

[71] Philip Graham Ryken, *1 Timothy*, Reformed Expository Commentary (Phillipsburg, N.J: P & R Pub, 2007), 130–131.

[72] Ibid., 131.

the 1 Timothy 3 passage because Paul mentions deacons again in the next verse. So, they believe this is talking about the wife of the deacon, of whom there is to be only one.

If it is about the wife of a deacon, Hughes and Chapell think "Paul is simply telling Timothy that a deacon must have a wife who has a respectability that matches his own, that his wife's qualifications are part and parcel of his qualifications for the office of deacon."[73]

Ryken helps us with this when he says,

> If the office of deaconess is not established in 1 Timothy 3, the diaconal ministry of women is certainly present elsewhere in the Bible. New Testament women frequently carried out diaconal ministry, in the broad sense of the word. Consider Dorcas, who was "full of good works and acts of charity (Acts 9:36). Or Lydia, who clothed the Philippians in purple (16:11-15). Or Tryphena and Tryphosa, women described as "workers in the Lord" (Rom. 16:12). Or especially Phoebe, who was "a patron of many" and is identified as "a servant of the church at Cenchreae"- literally, "a deaconess" (Rom. 16:1-2). To summarize, many New Testament women carried out diaconal ministry and one, at least, was called a "deaconess," even if she was not ordained as an officer of the church. The obvious conclusion is that whatever title they are given, women must be deeply involved in the mercy ministries of the church."[74]

At the very least, if a local church decides women can serve in the role of a deacon, they must have a respectability that matches

---

[73] R. Kent Hughes and Bryan Chapell, *1-2 Timothy and Titus: To Guard the Deposit* (Wheaton, IL: Crossway, 2012), 92.
[74] Ryken, *1 Timothy*, Reformed Expository Commentary, 131-132.

that of the male deacon.

Application Questions or Activities

1. Why are deacons to be honored and not seen or treated as lesser leaders? How do you view and treat those who serve in deacon roles as opposed to elder roles? Do you honor them equally?

2. If you are intending to serve as a deacon rather than an elder, how do you measure up to the qualifications? Or, if you are part of a group that chooses deacons, how do the individuals being considered measure up? Use the following assessment tool as a guide for your discussion about their qualifications.

The Qualities of a Deacon

A. A Good Reputation

1. One who is respected.

    ... are to be men worthy of respect (1 Tim. 3:8)

    ... who are known to be full of the Spirit and wisdom (Acts 6:3)

Weak				Strong
1	2	3	4	5

2. One who is blameless.

    ... with a clear conscience (1 Tim. 3:9)

    ... if there is nothing against them, let them serve as deacons (1 Tim. 3:10)

Weak				Strong
1	2	3	4	5

3. One who displays godliness in financial dealings.

    ... not pursuing dishonest gain (1 Tim. 3:8)

Weak				Strong

1	2	3	4	5

B. <u>Self-Control</u>

1. One who is not controlled by alcohol.

> ... *not indulging in much wine* (1 Tim. 3:8)

> ... *known to be full of the Spirit* (Acts 6:3)

Weak				Strong
1	2	3	4	5

2. One who is sincere.

> ... sincere (1 Tim. 3:8)

> *A Deacon's word must be trustworthy. He cannot say one thing to one person and something else to another. His yes must mean yes and his no, no.*

Weak				Strong
1	2	3	4	5

C. <u>A Healthy Home</u>

1. One who is faithful to his wife.

> ... *a deacon must be the husband of but one wife* (1 Tim. 3:12)

Weak				Strong
1	2	3	4	5

2. One who displays godly leadership at home.

> ... *and must manage his children and his household well* (1 Tim. 3:12)

Weak				Strong
1	2	3	4	5

3. One whose wife is living a godly life.

> ... *women worthy of respect*

> ... *not malicious talkers*

> ... *but temperate*

> ... *and trustworthy in everything* (1 Tim. 3:11)

Weak				Strong
1	2	3	4	5

D. A Mature Faith
1. One whose Christian maturity has been observed over time.
   ... who are known to be full of the Spirit and wisdom (Acts 6:3)

   *... they must first be tes*ted (1 Tim. 3:10)

Weak				Strong
1	2	3	4	5

2. One whose life is built on a solid Biblical foundation.
   ... they must keep hold of the deep truths of the faith with a clear conscience (1 Tim. 3:9)

Weak				Strong
1	2	3	4	5

3. As you review the qualities of a deacon outlined in the Bible, how do you measure up? Has weakness in any of these areas disqualified you from leadership at this time? Where do you need to keep growing? What do you need to do and what are you going to do to progress toward godliness in these areas?

Chapter 12: Leaving a Gospel Legacy

What do you want written on your gravestone? You are probably a long way from thinking about that, but what do you want people to say about your life? What do you want your wife to say about you? What do you want your children to say? What about your church family? What are you leaving behind? What will be the measure of your success?

This question is not to be asked out of vanity or from seeking self-glorification. This question should be asked with the same heart from which the words of John the Baptist came: *He must increase, but I must decrease. He who comes from above is above all. He who is of the earth belongs to the earth and speaks in an earthly way. He who comes from heaven is above all"* (John 3:30-31).

More important than our names and reputations, our material gains and our earthly success is that Christ be seen in and through us (Philippians 3:4-10). May the hope of our message, taught throughout our life and ministry, both through our deeds and by our tongues, live long after we die that we might continue to persuade many of its life-giving truth! Would that we leave a gospel-legacy.

Each time we stand in front of our listeners and long for their approval, whenever we are tempted to take partial credit for someone's salvation, when we are discouraged because our church isn't big enough, or our words are not quoted by others, or our online content hasn't gone viral, we need to remind ourselves of the words of Paul in Philippians 3:3-16.

For we are the circumcision, who worship by the Spirit of God and glory in Christ Jesus and put no confidence in the flesh— though I myself have reason for confidence in the flesh also. If anyone else thinks he has reason for confidence in the flesh, I have more: circumcised on the eighth day, of the people of Israel, of the tribe of Benjamin, a Hebrew of Hebrews; as to the law, a Pharisee; as to zeal, a persecutor of the church; as to righteousness under the law, blameless. But whatever gain I had, I counted as loss for the sake of Christ. Indeed, I count everything as loss because of the surpassing worth of knowing Christ Jesus my Lord. For his sake I have suffered the loss of all things and count them as rubbish, in order that I may gain Christ and be found in him, not having a righteousness of my own that comes from the law, but that which comes through faith in Christ, the righteousness from God that depends on faith— that I may know him and the power of his resurrection, and may share his sufferings, becoming like him in his death, that by any means possible I may attain the resurrection from the dead.

Not that I have already obtained this or am already perfect, but I press on to make it my own, because Christ Jesus has made me his own. Brothers, I do not consider that I have made it my own. But one thing I do: forgetting what lies behind and straining forward to what lies ahead, I press on toward the goal for the prize of the upward call of God in Christ Jesus. Let those of us who are mature think this way, and if in anything you think otherwise, God will reveal that also to you. Only let us hold true to what we have attained.

Paul begins by emphasizing that as believers we are those who *"worship by the Spirit of God and glory of Christ Jesus and put no confidence in the flesh* (v. 3). He then makes a list all the things he could brag about from an earthly perspective. He had reputation and status, religious zeal, and though the text doesn't state it, almost certainly some level of wealth. Paul calls himself a *Hebrew of Hebrews* (v. 5). By human standards, he was blameless and pious (v. 6). He was successful and popular among his peers as he sought to eliminate the followers of Christ (v. 6; see also Acts 7:54-8:3; Gal. 1:13).

But in verse 7, Paul considers *it all as loss for the sake of Christ.*

Why? Because Paul became far more interested in *the surpassing worth of knowing Christ Jesus*. He looked at all his accomplishments and said, *For his sake I have suffered the loss of all things and count them as rubbish, in order that I may gain Christ and be found in him* (verses 8-9). Christ reorients Paul's focus from personal gain and self-righteousness to a pursuit of Christ and the holiness he gives.

After humbly confessing that he hasn't achieved this goal or obtained perfection (verse 12), Paul states his life-objective in verses 13 and 14: *forgetting what lies behind and straining forward to what lies ahead, I press on toward the goal for the prize of the upward call of God in Christ Jesus*. He immediately follows these words with: *Let those of us who are mature think this way, and if in anything you think otherwise, God will reveal that also to you.*

Whenever we find ourselves pursuing something other than *the goal for the prize of the upward call of God in Christ Jesus,* whenever we are seeking our own glory or chasing our own ambitions, we are not thinking maturely. We are not acting as mature believers. Further, Paul is warning us that God will reveal our immaturity.

God's revelation of our immaturity must drive us to the cross, causing us to repent, and thereafter enjoy the good gifts of God's grace and forgiveness. Only through repentance can God reorient our hearts to our primary mission as God's children, and as the men God has chosen to lead his church.

In Your Life

In 2 Timothy 4:7 Paul wrote, *I have fought the good fight, I have finished the race, I have kept the faith.* In this verse, Paul uses three phrases that sum up his life's accomplishments.[75]

First, he says *I have fought the good fight.* It is very important to

---

[75] Adapted from the book *The Power of His Presence*: a year of devotions from the writings of Ray Stedman; compiled by Mark Mitchell.

see he did not say, "I have fought a good fight," as he is often quoted as saying. If he had said that, it would be expressing a view of how well he had done. It would be boasting: "I've fought a good fight. I've worked hard, I've hung in there and done the right thing." But that is not what he says. He says, "I have fought <u>the</u> good fight," meaning the significant fight, the great battle that life had presented to him.

Second, Paul says, *I have finished the race.* In Philippians 3 he describes that race: *Forgetting what is behind and straining toward what is ahead, I press on toward the goal to win the prize for which God has called me heavenward in Christ Jesus* (Philippians 3:13-14). The race, of course, is the Christian life itself, which is lived moment by moment, just as a race is run step by step.

The question is whether you live each step in the flesh or in the Spirit, whether you are walking in the power of the new life you have from Christ or whether you are still running in the old ways of thinking, the old self-centered, fleshly, self-serving attitudes. Every moment is either contributing to reaching the goal for the prize or delaying it, wasting time in the flesh. Christians are called to run that race.

Third, Paul says, *I have kept the faith.* "The faith" is the whole body of truth that is involved in the gospel, what he calls in 1 Corinthians "God's secret wisdom" (1 Corinthians 2:7). This wisdom is totally different from the wisdom of this world. It is the truth that God tells us about ourselves and about himself, about this world and why it is the way it is. It is the truth about the power of evil, "the secret power of lawlessness" (2 Thessalonians 2:7), and "the mystery of godliness" (1 Timothy 3:16) with which we can counteract evil. That is "the faith" that Paul is talking about.

On the very edge of eternity, he can say of himself, "I have kept the faith. I have not lost any of the good deposit that God has entrusted to me." He has guarded it as a treasure, and he tells Timothy in turn to "guard the good deposit that was entrusted to you" (2 Timothy 1:14). Paul has kept this treasure from being mistreated or distorted by those who would try to twist it and use it for their own purposes. Thus, he has "kept the faith."

What will be said about your life?

In Your Family

What will you leave behind in your family? If you keep going the direction you are going in the management of your household, what will you leave as a gospel legacy?

We trust you will take a careful look at the direction of your household leadership so that you will leave behind wise children and grandchildren who will succeed in walking with God. These may be your actual children and grandchildren, or if you are childless, they will be those you have been a part of discipling throughout your life. Proverbs 4:10-13 says,

> *Hear, my son, and accept my words, that the years of your life may be many. I have taught you the way of wisdom; I have led you in the paths of uprightness. When you walk, your step will not be hampered, and if you run, you will not stumble. Keep hold of instruction; do not let go; guard her, for she is your life.*

Proverbs 13:1 adds, *A wise son hears his father's instruction, but a scoffer does not listen to rebuke.*

We trust you will leave behind children and grandchildren who will bring you joy. The writer of Proverbs speaks to this more than once:

> *A wise son makes a glad father, but a foolish man despises his mother* (Proverbs 15:20).
>
> *The father of the righteous will greatly rejoice; he who fathers a wise son will be glad in him* (Proverbs 23:24).

My son, give me your heart, and let your eyes observe my ways (Proverbs 23:26).

Discipline your son, and he will give you rest; he will give delight to your heart (Proverbs 29:17).

In Your Ministry

I (Richard) have adopted this prayer, from the Valley of Vision, as my own. I encourage you adopt it as your own as well:

Blessed Spirit of God,

Four evils attend my ministry —

[1]The devil treads me down by

discouragement and shame

arising from coldness in private meditation.

[2]Carelessness possesses me

from natural dullness and dimness of spirit;

because in the past I have met with success

and been highly regarded,

so that it does not matter if I have now

failed.

[3]Infirmities and weakness are mine

from want of spiritual light, life and power,

so that souls have not been helped,

and I have not felt thee to be near.

[4]Lack of success has followed even when

I have done my best.

But thou hast shown me that the glory of everything

that is sanctified to do good

is not seen in itself,

but in the source of its sanctification.

Thus my end in preaching is to know Christ,

and impart his truth;

my principle in preaching is Christ himself,
  whom I trust,
    for in him is fullness of spirit and strength;
    my comfort in preaching is to do all for him.
 Help me in my work to grow more humble,
  to pick something out of all providences
    to that end,
  to joy in thee and loathe myself,
  to keep my life, being, soul, and body
    only for thee,
  to carry my heart to thee in love and delight,
  to see all my grace in thee, coming from thee,
  to walk with thee in endearment.
 Then, whether I succeed or fail,
  nought matters but thee alone.[76]

Every honest elder or pastor will admit their ministry is plagued at some point by the same four evils that this puritan pastor confessed: shame and discouragement from a distant personal relationship with God; weakness and atrophy, which comes from lack of spiritual sustenance; pride, which leads to complacency; and failure despite best efforts. Make this prayer your own that you might make war with these enemies in your own heart and ministry, a war which, only in his power, will you ever win.

We acknowledge and remind ourselves that the power of our ministry rests not in us, but in Christ. Our goal in ministry is to know Christ and share his good news. In our preaching and teaching, our focus is Christ himself. Our joy and comfort in the struggles of ministry is to do it all for him.

---

[76] Arthur Bennett, *The Valley of Vision: A Collection of Puritan Prayers & Devotions* (Edinburgh: Banner of Truth Trust, 2002), 336–337.

If you are going to leave behind a gospel-legacy rather than a legacy of shame, discouragement, pride, and/or failure you too will have to regularly acknowledge and remind yourself that the only thing that matters is Christ alone.

What will you leave behind in your ministry? What will your years of service be remembered by? After you are gone, what will be the impact of your life on this country? Will you leave a gospel legacy?

We trust your life will serve as a model for other men. Paul told Timothy, *Let no one despise you for your youth, but set the believers an example in speech, in conduct, in love, in faith, in purity* (1 Timothy 4:12). He added, *Practice these things, devote yourself to them, so that all may see your progress. Keep a close watch on yourself and on the teaching. Persist in this, for by so doing you will save both yourself and your hearers* (4:15-16).

We trust you will invest in other men. We trust that you will *be strengthened by the grace that is in Christ Jesus, and what you have heard from me in the presence of many witnesses entrust to faithful men who will be able to teach others also* (2 Timothy 2:1-2).

What does this mean for you? It means you need to anchor men in the teaching of the Scripture as it applies to every area of their lives. You must teach men to be the best possible husbands. You must assist fathers to assume responsibility for their children and model the faith for them. You must participate in and encourage the training of other promising young men who are called to leadership within the church.

Five Commands from 1 Corinthians 16:13-14

Paul says, *Be watchful, stand firm in the faith, act like men, be strong. Let all that you do be done in love.*

We pray that these five commands will set the direction of

your life, impact your household, and inform your leadership.

- *Be watchful.* Be on your guard. You have an enemy who desires to ruin your life. Watch your own life. Watch the lives of your family.

- *Stand firm in the faith* – Anchor yourself in the gospel and its implications for your life. Be a man who clings to the Word of God and continually goes to for answers and to hear the voice of God. Be a man who seeks the heart of God through His Word and not one who tells God what he should think and do.

- *Act like men.* Be courageous as you face sinful behavior in your life and the lives of others around you. Be courageous as you face the teaching of wrong doctrine. Be courageous as you lead your family and the church family toward godliness.

- *Be strong* – Don't cave into what everyone else is saying or doing. Don't just rely on your own strength, but trust in the power of the Holy Spirit. Allow Him to fill and control you. Allow Him to bring strength to your weakness. Trust that His grace is sufficient for every need.

- *Let all be done in love.* No matter who you interact with or what you face as the issue of the day, be a man who is known as a lover of people! Love your wife. Love your children. Love your extended family. Love your grandchildren. Love your church family. Love your neighbors.

Though we have said it before, we say it again, Christ has given us the gift of repentance when we fail. Repentance is the conduit through which God transfers his grace and forgiveness to sinners. When we fail at the exhortations and commands given to us throughout the Scripture, we can freely and boldly go before the throne of grace, asking God to forgive and to remove our guilt because of Christ's work on the cross. This is true for those whom we care for, and it is true for us as their elders, pastors, and ministry leaders.

Our gospel-legacy does not depend on our getting everything right all the time. The reason the gospel is necessary is because it is impossible for us get everything right all the time. Our gospel legacy depends on our willingness to admit our weakness, confess our sin and our readiness to follow the leading of the Holy Spirit.

We rest in Christ and him alone for our forgiveness. We rest in Christ and him alone for our strength. We rest in Christ and him alone to make us worthy of his calling. We rest in Christ and him alone to make our calling effective. He and he alone is the object of our affection, and he and he alone is the worthy recipient of our worship and praise. He is our message and our mission. He is the reason we love those around us and the source of love we draw from that we might love them well. He is the reason we say what we say, do what we do.

Conclusion and Summary

To sum up this chapter; and this book, we remind you that:

- You have a glorious Redeemer. May he outshine you in everything you do and speak. May his glory and grace be seen in you so that everyone who knows you, lives with you, does business with you, and worships with you would see the glorious character of God through you.

- You have been given an enormous responsibility to model Christlikeness to those under your care – your family, your friends, your neighbors, your colleagues, and your church family. Love them well and do not forsake, oppress, or betray them.

- You have a noble calling as an elder and church leader. Live it in every relationship and every corner of your life.

- You have an urgent and important message of hope and eternal life. Know it thoroughly and intimately and carefully proclaim it with your life and your tongue.

- You have a significant responsibility to learn, teach and guard sound doctrine. As an elder or pastor, continue to be a student of the Bible so that you may clearly proclaim God's Word without being ashamed of how you studied and taught his precious truths and promises.

- You have a gracious Saviour who both gives you all that you need to follow this path and forgives you when you fail. Trust in him with all your heart. Lean on him instead of your own understanding and strength.

Overall, manage your household well!

<u>Application Questions or Activities</u>

1. When the Lord calls you to be with him in glory, what do you want people to say about the gospel as seen in your life?

2. If you were to stand before the Lord today, in what areas of your life and ministry would he say, "Well done!" In what areas might do you still need to grow?

3. What do you need to do to *Be watchful, stand firm in the faith, act like men, be strong. Let all that you do be done in love.* Be specific as you develop a strategic plan that outlines the places you need to grow along with the steps you could take towards that growth.

Bibliography

Alcorn, Randy C. *The Purity Principle*. Sisters, Or: Multnomah
Publishers, 2003.

Bennett, Arthur. *The Valley of Vision: A Collection of Puritan Prayers
& Devotions*. Edinburgh: Banner of Truth Trust, 2002.

Garcia, Lauren. "Special Needs: Defining and Understanding the
4 Types." *Care.Com Resources*, March 18, 2022. Accessed June
29, 2022. https://www.care.com/c/types-of-special-needs/.

Grudem, Wayne A. *Systematic Theology: An Introduction to Biblical
Doctrine (2nd Edition)*. Second Edition., 2020.

Guthrie, Donald, ed. *The New Bible Commentary: Revised*. Grand
Rapids, Mich: Eerdmans, 1973.

Hughes, R. Kent, and Bryan Chapell. *1-2 Timothy and Titus: To
Guard the Deposit*. Wheaton, IL: Crossway, 2012.

Keller, Timothy. *Prayer: Experiencing Awe and Intimacy with God*.
New York: Penguin Group, 2016.

Köstenberger, Andreas J., and David W. Jones. *God, Marriage &
Family: Rebuilding the Biblical Foundation*. Wheaton, Ill:
Crossway Books, 2004.

Kroeker, Daryl. *Gripping the Essentials: A Brief Handbook of
Theology*. Surrey, BC: WorldServe Ministries, 2022.

Louw, J. P., and Eugene A. Nida, eds. *Greek-English Lexicon of the
New Testament: Based on Semantic Domains*. 1st ed. New York,
NY, USA: United Bible Societies, 1988.

Moody, Diane. *Confessions of a Prayer Slacker*. Second Edition.
OBT Bookz. Kindle Edition, 2016.

Ortlund, Dane Calvin. *Deeper: Real Change for Real Sinners*. Union. Wheaton, Illinois: Crossway, 2021.

Piper, John. "How Much Does God Want Me to Care for My Physical Body?" *Desiring God*, August 7, 2009. Accessed May 24, 2022. https://www.desiringgod.org/interviews/how-much-does-god-want-me-to-care-for-my-physical-body.

————. "How to Deal with the Guilt of Sexual Failure for the Glory of Christ and His Global Cause." *Desiring God*. Last modified January 4, 2007. Accessed May 25, 2022. https://www.desiringgod.org/messages/how-to-deal-with-the-guilt-of-sexual-failure-for-the-glory-of-christ-and-his-global-cause.

————. "The Word of Faith That We Proclaim, Part 1." *Desiring God*. Last modified May 18, 2003. Accessed May 23, 2022. https://www.desiringgod.org/messages/the-word-of-faith-that-we-proclaim-part-1.

————. "How Do I Not Provoke My Children?" *Desiring God*, n.d. Accessed May 25, 2022. https://www.desiringgod.org/interviews/how-do-i-not-provoke-my-children.

————. "Topics for Conversation When a Man and a Woman Are Considering Marriage." *Desiring God*, January 1, 1995. Accessed May 24, 2022. https://www.desiringgod.org/articles/topics-for-conversation-when-a-man-and-a-woman-are-considering-marriage.

Ryken, Philip Graham. *1 Timothy*. Reformed Expository Commentary. Phillipsburg, N.J: P & R Pub, 2007.

Tennent, Timothy C. *For the Body: Recovering a Theology of Gender, Sexuality, and the Human Body*. Grand Rapids, Michigan,

[Franklin, Tennessee]: Zondervan Reflective ; [Seedbed Publishing], 2020.

Walton, Sarah. "To Parents with Special Needs." *Desiring God,* July 14, 2017. Accessed June 29, 2022. https://www.desiringgod.org/articles/to-parents-with-special-needs.

Ware, Bruce A. *Father, Son, and Holy Spirit: Relationships, Roles, and Relevance.* Wheaton, Ill: Crossway Books, 2005.

Whitney, Donald S. *Praying the Bible.* Wheaton, Illinois: Crossway, 2015.

Meet the Authors

Daryl Kroeker

After 40 years in local church pastoral ministry, Daryl joined WorldServe Ministries where he started WorldServe Bible College and now serves as its Academic Director. This program takes Bible college training to pastors and church leaders in various parts of the world where access to biblical training is restricted for various reasons. WorldServe Bible College is currently working with students in 15 different countries.

Daryl is also part of the team at Millar College of the Bible where he teaches on the Sunnybrae Campus and gives leadership to the Master of Biblical Studies program.

Daryl and Tamara have been married 41 years and have been blessed with two children and twelve grandchildren.

Other books by Daryl Kroeker include:

- *Beyond Ourselves: How Can the Unreached Be Reached* (2014)
- *Psalm 119: Stirring a Love for the Word* (2019)
- *Gripping the Essentials: A Brief Handbook of Theology* (2022)

Richard Magill

Richard has been serving in vocational pastoral and counselling ministry for approximately fifteen years and beyond this has served as volunteer in the church for many more years. He is currently serving as Director of Redemption Counselling in Salmon Arm, BC Canada, and Counselling Pastor of Shuswap Community Church. In addition to biblical counselling, his duties include lay-counsellor and discipleship training, benevolence, pastoral care and visitation, and pulpit supply.

During his years of counseling, Richard has counseled several pastors in emotional, relational, spiritual, and career crises. He also serves as pastoral mentor for M.Div. students at Northwest Baptist Seminary and has served as intern supervisor for 4th year students at Millar College of the Bible.

Richard grew up in the southeastern United States but has lived in and served communities in the Mid Atlantic, Midwest, and the deep south prior to coming to Canada. He now lives in the interior of beautiful British Columbia with his bride of 27 years and an incredibly high-maintenance beagle named Shadow.